"Portrait of Arne", Photograph by *Don Wilson*, 2014.

Published by Studio Dreamshare Press
Chapeau, Quebec
www.studiodreamsharepress.com

Edited by Cameron Montgomery
Layout and Design by Rose Bennett
Studio Dreamshare Press

Library and Archives Canada Cataloguing in Publication
Smelle, Nate, 1976–
'Twas a Sunny Day / by Nate Smelle; featuring art and poetry by Arne Roosman.

Includes bibliographical references.

ISBN 978-1-989832-15-8

Smelle, Nate, 1976—Biography.

Roosman, Arne—Illustrations.

Artists—Canada—Biography.
I. Roosman, Arne, 1932– II. Title.

Poets—Canada—Biography.

First Edition, 2025

Cover Art:
"Simcoe on the Lake", *Arne Roosman*, watercolour on paper, 1960.

'TWAS A SUNNY DAY

Written by Nate Smelle
With Art and Poetry by Arne Roosman

Tee hääd, tee kurja, kõik teed endale.[1]
- **Estonian Proverb**

Whether you do good or do evil, you do it to yourself.

This book is printed in black and white to preserve accessibility and affordability.

We invite you to view the complete collection of images from *'Twas a Sunny Day* in full colour through our online gallery.

You can visit studiodreamsharepress.com to view the online gallery.

Through this digital gallery, you can explore full-colour reproductions of Roosman's paintings and drawings referenced in the text, and exclusive content curated to accompany the book.

THE FAYRITALE MY MOTER NEVER TOLD ME!
DID SHE FORGET? OR NEVER HEARD OF IT.?

MY HIDDEN HEART
NO NEST!
A NIGHTINGALE
NO CATHEDRAL
TO CARRY A TUNE.
NOW I'LL CHOOSE
THE TROPICS
MY SUNSHINE
"ROBINETTES"
TO WINGED HIGHTS
BEYOND THE PILLOWS
OF HAPPY CHILDRENS
DREAMFUL NIGHTS -
ALL ASLEEP.

ON MY
HOME TURF
I A PRINCE
A ROBIN.
AWAY AS WELL
NO PROBLEM!
ON PALM
COVERED SURF
ON MY
BEDPOST
I STAND
A BERNSTEIN
A LEONARD
TO BOOST.

A CROW'S
NEST MINE
IN THE DARKFEST
FARAWAY
FOREST
TO CARRY ROYAL
CROAKS
IS NOT A HOAKS
YOU LEFT THE
WALKYRIANS TO
CRY BEHIND MY
FEATHERED TAIL.
TOOK CARE OF
THE FARTS!

"Three Little Birds", *Arne Roosman*, ink on paper, 2023.

TABLE OF CONTENTS

"Self-Portrait of Arne and Uku", *Arne Roosman,* mixed media on paper, 2014.

Artist's Prologue

As a silent cloud, all words.
Two carry a sentence reaching for the blue beyond.
Keeping my past in focus,
I owe much too many a writer of current concerns and fears.
The Trumps, Musks, and Putins,
colouring and feeding the political Rainbow of blood and tears.
Thanks to Rachel Carson for her not so Silent Spring,
it burdens one with guilt
when turning on the noisy lawn mower to cut the lovely grass.
Harold R. Johnsons', The Bjorkin Sagas,
to bring a whiff of Scandinavia onto these pages,
and Joseph Boesberg's Kujamae Kroonika
to reconnect with my maternal grandfather and centuries of long ago.
Many thanks to Nate, Ronnie, and Rose for making all this possible.

– Arne Roosman

FORWARD

"102, Ronnie," said Arne on my latest visit. "That's what we're working on– 102." Arne Roosman means his age. Born in 1932 in the Bloodlands during one of the world's bloodlustiest times, Arne is no stranger to beating the odds. His beautiful soul is bursting with indomitable life, and I'm certain Arne will live as long as he wants to, including to 102.

Arne Roosman has lived a poignant and fascinating life so far, and he wears it in the sparkle of his ice blue eyes, the way he rolls his rrr's, his fashionable self-styling, sitting at the kitchen table, listening to CBC Radio and painting scenes from Ragnarok. This man is one of the greatest I have ever known, an inspiration for my own art and the most clever conversationalist. The man cannot suffer from boredom, for his interests are deep and varied. He is not bogged down by trivial malaise; he has survived unspeakable horrors, and takes pleasure in the joys of good food, good company, and good books. And of course, art. Arne is one of the most talented artists I have ever worked with. His prolific body of work spans haunting scenes from a strange childhood, to stirring portraits of beautiful women infused with mythological motifs, to meditations on music; Arne mounted an exhibition called "Touching Jazz" at my art gallery Studio Dreamshare, where Canadian Jazz Hall of Fame pianist Armas Maiste performed at the opening.

Arne and I are separated in age by half a century; he has never, and will never use the internet, and he casually mentions things in conversation like enjoying Ella Fitzgerald live at a jazz bar in Stockholm in the 50s, but his intellect cuts through time and technobabble like a knife. Arne has an uncanny ability to distill life down to its trembling core and cut straight to the heart of the matter. He understands that art can be an antidote to fascism, that painting your way through trauma can be powerful medicine.

The day we met, I knew we would be friends for life. Of course, such a person has many wonderful friendships; indeed, Arne always has an entourage of impressive people surrounding him. Some connections he has maintained for decades, forged in DP camps in the chaos after WWII, others are bright young artists, writers, models, and activists, and everyone of any age with an ounce of creativity and intelligence is able to see Arne's brilliance shining like a beacon of light and wants to be his friend.

I love Arne, and Nate has allowed me to write a few words about him here. What a joy and an honour to write a forward for a book about a dear friend.

I met Canadian journalist Nate Smelle through Arne. Nate is a bright and passionate writer bursting with ideas and reflections on the state of the world. Everyone's relationship with Arne is a bit different, like many portraits of the same subject. Nate is Arne's debate partner, drinking buddy and dear friend, and the book sings this song.

Nate's earnest telling of his friendship with Arne and the rich stories they have shared is the bedrock of this book exploring the continuing rise of fascism in our times. As a journalist living on the scorching edge of our swiftly tilting planet, Nate has the ability to pull threads of news from around the world together, and compare them to Arne's rich life experience. As a master artist, Arne has a uniquely illustrative way of describing the world in colour, shape and texture. Nate has done an excellent job of drawing this artful dialogue into the book.

As in art, so in life; movements rise and fall, and the longer we live, the more patterns we see. In his long and storied life, Arne has seen many resurgences. The Nazis, the Holocaust, the Bloodlands, the Molotov-Ribbentrop Line– these were stories Arne did not want to experience again, and yet he has felt the dark echoes rising of late, from the ashes of the millions, rearing the ugly head of fascism in the invasion of Ukraine, the rise of Musk and Putin and Trump. Arne fled decimated Europe for the wilds of rural Ontario, moving to the most remote little place he could find to make a home with his love Liina, and a lifetime later, he faces yet another homeland endangered as Trump threatens to make Canada the 51st state of the U.S.A.

Are we doomed to repeat the past? Or can the good people of earth forge a future that is for and by the people for real?

These and other questions are discussed at Arne's table. Pull up a chair. Fill your glass. Let us begin.

Cameron Montgomery, Ph.D.

Studio Dreamshare Press

FIVE MONTHS AND FIVE YEARS

"The way to right wrongs is to turn the light of truth upon them."
– Ida B. Wells-Barnett, 1892

'Twas a sunny day as I headed south on that familiar stretch of Highway 62 between L'Amable and Coe Hill to visit my friend, the Estonian Canadian artist, Arne Roosman. It was just before noon, less than five hours before the setting sun would welcome the longest night of 2024. Somewhat accidentally, Arne and I have established a custom of getting together to celebrate on the Solstices. Also by chance, it was a conversation Arne and I had on the night of the Winter Solstice in 2019 that inspired us to set out on this adventure through the past, present, and future, which we have been on for the past six years as we put together his memoir.

I was up for more than 48 hours wrestling with this introduction, and I was in no shape to be behind the wheel. However, considering my deadline with the publishers at Studio Dreamshare was already 24 hours in the rearview mirror, and the fact I have been struggling to turn out these final pages since I handed the first draft over to them last spring, nothing short of an atomic bomb landing in the heart of Bancroft's business district was going to stop me from taking a seat at Arne's kitchen table, to go over my notes with him on this day.

Writing a handful of pages is not usually a huge chore for me. I've had the privilege of covering municipal politics in Ontario for more than a decade, so I know about taking a pile of words mostly about nothing and whittling them down to what needs to be said. What makes this dreaded introduction so different is that instead of trying to say as little as possible that will stir up the pitchforks and torches, as the majority of our elected officials tend to do, Arne and I have been putting all the cards on the table.

These pages have presented such a unique challenge for me because of the lightning speed flurry of world-altering events that have taken place since I began my dialogue with the artist in the early hours of the winter of 2019. The time between the winter Solstices of 2019 and 2024 has left me fully and completely rattled by the rush.

A little less than a month after I submitted this book to the publisher, my plan to provide the reader with context for Arne's story by putting together a few final reflections on the process of writing 'Twas a Sunny Day went out the window. On July 13, 2024, while most of the world's attention was drawn to a mass shooting and highly suspicious alleged assassination attempt on Donald Trump at a MAGA rally in Butler, Pennsylvania, I found myself 34,000+ feet above Doha, Qatar, en route to Jakarta, Indonesia to work on a documentary film series for the next five weeks. The news arrived through a text from my friend, informing me of the chaos unfolding in real time on every major news outlet throughout North America.

It was at this moment, as I hovered there in the sky reading her message, that the gravity of the situation unfolding in the United States of America began to settle in. Along with this newfound awareness came a creeping realization that the gears of the human history-making machine were turning way too fast and furiously for me to properly process the convergence of events taking place in relation to the Arne Roosman experience, and our then four-and-a-half-year examination of the dangerous absurdity of the resurgence of far-right fascist movements worldwide.

In the five months leading up to this delightfully bitter cold and bright morning of the 2024 winter Solstice, we witnessed a staggering number of transformative world events that seem to have rendered many, including myself, utterly stunned. Upon taking a quick snapshot of this brief period of time between July and December 2024 to get my bearings before writing these critical last words, my anxiety immediately spiked when it hit me how sinister and unstable our world is becoming every single day. There is no longer any time to really take in and thoroughly analyze the facts.

In retrospect, I think the America Last oligarchy discovered during the COVID-19 pandemic, that 'the people', the working class, or whatever you want to call the consumers responsible for blindly delivering them such grotesque wealth, have realized that the system is rigged to make the richest richer by keeping everyone else in line and in love with their chains. Fascism—a system that flourishes when might is always right and 'alternative facts' hold more weight than the truth—is fast becoming the last viable option to stay on the top of the pyramid. The soft complicity of the mainstream media is essential to this lopsided status quo.

In the hours and days immediately following the first apparent attempt on Trump's life, there were very few serious questions about the highly suspicious events of that day. When I returned home from Indonesia in mid-August, I found out that Arne also shared my concerns about what happened that day at the MAGA rally in Butler, Pennsylvania. The big question on both of our minds, and many others', was and still is: how was Thomas Matthew Crooks, a gawky, 20-year old registered Republican with no ties to the military, able to slip by the Secret Service, climb onto a rooftop within sight and shooting distance of the former president, and fire several shots?

The entire scene reeked of a poorly staged high school production of a scene from the classic 2010 Robert Rodriguez and Ethan Maniquis film, *Machete*. Although many of Trump's speeches could have been torn from those delivered by one of the film's main villains— a corrupt Texas State Senator John McLaughlin, played by Robert De Niro—the clip that immediately came to mind when I saw the footage of the incident online, was one in which an assassination attempt on Senator McLaughlin is staged to boost his poll numbers. But that was a movie, and appears to have happened on that day in Butler, Pennsylvania resulted in the killing of both Corey Comperatore, a 50-year-old Trump supporter, and the shooter, Crooks.

Before anyone in the media could really shine a light on and dig into this assault on democracy, the turf upon which the campaign was taking place shifted dramatically on July 21, when incumbent U.S.A. President Joe Biden announced he was ending his bid for re-election. This announcement came just hours before Vice President Kamala Harris, who had been serving as Biden's running mate, declared her own candidacy for the presidency.

As Democrats in the U.S.A. were rallying around their new candidate at the top of the ticket, unusually heavy rains brought on by the climate crisis—arguably a much greater threat to our existence than the outcome of any election—triggered landslides in the Gofa Zone of South Ethiopia, killing 257 people. A few days later on July 30, torrential rains provoked a series of landslides in the villages of Punjirimattom, Mundakkai, Chooralmala, and Vellarimala in the Wayanad District of India that buried another 334 people alive. In the weeks to follow a group of scientists known as the World Weather Attribution determined through the use of climate models that the 15 centimeters (5.91 inches) of rain that fell in the area over a 24-hour period between July 29-30 was 10 per cent more intense because of the year-over-year rise in Earth's temperature due to carbon emissions.

As the world was still grappling with the rescue and recovery efforts taking place in response to these climate disasters on July 30, Fuad Shukr, a Lebanese militant leader and senior member of Hezbollah was assassinated in an Israeli airstrike on an apartment building in the Lebanese capital of Beirut, that also killed Iranian military adviser Milad Bedi, five Lebanese civilians, including two children, and wounded 80 others. The assassination was said to be a retaliatory response to Shukr's alleged involvement in a rocket attack that killed 12 Syrian Druze children and teenagers three days earlier

9

in Majdal Shams, an Israeli-occupied town in Golan Heights. The next day, Ismail Haniyeh, the leader of Hamas, was assassinated in Tehran by another Israeli strike.

Back in the U.S.A., as violence continued to spread throughout the Middle East, candidate Trump was stoking the flames of hatred on the campaign trail. During an interview at the National Association of Black Journalists' annual convention, Trump again showed his true colours when he accused his Democratic opponent Kamala Harris of "turning Black" to gain votes.

This controversy came on the heels of a wave of race riots in the United Kingdom, sparked by a mass stabbing in Southport, England that killed three children. Anti-immigrant groups in the U.K. exploited the tragedy, spreading misinformation that fueled the violence, which escalated into racist attacks, arson, and looting. Trump's Nazi-curious billionaire backer and professional internet troll Elon Musk used his platform to pour more gas on the situation, tweeting:

"Civil war is inevitable."

By early August, as the U.K. riots subsided, Kamala Harris was officially confirmed as the Democratic Party's presidential nominee, with Minnesota Governor Tim Walz announced as her vice-presidential pick. On August 11, Ukraine launched a cross-border offensive into Russia's Kursk Oblast, forcing the evacuation of over 76 000 Russian civilians. This escalation of violence came amidst other global flashpoints, such as the massacre of 600 civilians in Burkina Faso by a far-right jihadist group with ties to al-Qaeda on August 24, and the Israel Defense Forces' preemptive strikes in southern Lebanon the next day.

On September 6, war criminal and former U.S.A. vice president Dick Cheney and his daughter, the former Congresswoman Liz Cheney, threw their support behind U.S.A. Vice President Harris' campaign. The Harris campaign received another boost on September 10 following the second televised presidential debate on ABC News, in which Trump was caught live on television spreading a false conspiracy theory about Haitian immigrants eating people's pets.

Although a shot was never fired, less than a week later on September 15, there was another alleged assassination attempt on then former U.S.A. president and Republican Party nominee Donald Trump at the Trump International Golf Club in West Palm Beach, Florida. Two days later, 32 people were killed and some 4000 more injured in Lebanon when explosives were planted in pagers and walkie talkies—presumably by Israel—that were believed to be used by Hezbollah militants and medics.

The death toll from the climate crisis continued its climb on September 26 when Hurricane Helene made landfall in Florida, killing 236 people. This same day, Trump outsourced his on-the-ground campaigning in swing states to Elon Musk's America PAC (Lowell 2024). Seventy-two hours later, the far-right Freedom Party secured a victory for racists and fascists everywhere in the 2024 Austrian Legislative election—the first far-right win since the Second World War. Shining a light on the Nazi roots of the far-right party, an article published by the Anadolu Agency states: "The FPO was founded in 1956 by Anton Reinthaller, an Austrian Nazi who had previously served as a lieutenant general in the SS, the Nazis' paramilitary wing, as well as a member of the Nazi parliament until the end of WWII" (Kiyagan 2024).

In a last-ditch effort to salvage Trump's floundering campaign, on October 7, Musk began bribing voters by offering them a $47 'reward' for signing his petition. According to Forbes, Musk claimed that he was offering the payments for the successful referral of a registered swing state voter to sign the petition "to show support for free speech and the right to bear arms" (Roeloffs 2024). Three days later he increased the 'reward' to $100 and pledged to give $1-Million to a random signer each day. Many questioned the legality of the "richest" man in the world paying off registered voters, including Derek Muller, an election law expert who teaches at Notre Dame Law School who explained in a CNN report: "When you start limiting prizes or giveaways to only registered voters or only people who have voted, that's where bribery concerns arise. By limiting a giveaway only to registered voters, it looks like you're giving cash for voter registration" (Cohen 2024). By October 27, the racist rhetoric that has become synonymous with the MAGA movement was making headlines again after a rally at Madison Square Gardens in New York City, when one of Trump's guest speakers described Puerto Rico as a "floating island of garbage" (Bohannon 2024). The event reeked of the American Nazi rally held at the same venue in 1939, with Trump planting the same seeds of division is idol Adolf did throughout the Second World War. *The Guardian* observed the similarities between the two rallies in its coverage, acknowledging that: "Nine days out from the election, Trump used the rally in New York to repeat his claim that he is fighting 'the enemy from within' and again promised to launch 'the largest deportation program in American history', amid incoherent ramblings about ending a phone call with a 'very, very important person' so he could watch one of Elon Musk's rockets land. ...The event at Madison Square Garden, in the center of Manhattan, had drawn comparisons to an infamous Nazi rally held at the arena in 1939. Tim Walz, Kamala Harris's running mate, said there was a 'direct parallel' between the two events, and the Democratic National Committee projected images on the outside of the building on Sunday repeating claims from Trump's former chief of staff that Trump had "praised Hitler" (Gabbatt & Pilkington 2024).

The increasingly hateful tone of Trump's speeches reached new extremes a few days later during a campaign stop on Halloween, when he threatened violence against Liz Cheney. Calling her a "radical war hawk," he boasted to his supporters, "Let's put her with the rifle standing there with nine barrels shooting at her. OK, let's see how she feels about it. You know, when the guns are trained on her face" (Howard 2024).

Without any concern for the fountain of septage spewing from Trump's lips, the climate crisis struck again on October 29—this time in Spain—when record-breaking rains caused widespread flooding throughout the eastern and southern part of the country, killing 231 people (Spanish Government 2024). Explaining how the climate crisis worsened the severity of the floods in Spain, Dr. Friederike Otto, the leader of an international group of scientists studying the role that global heating plays in extreme weather events, told BBC that there was "No doubt about it, these explosive downpours were intensified by climate change. ...With every fraction of a degree of fossil fuel warming, the atmosphere can hold more moisture, leading to heavier bursts of rainfall" (McGrath 2024).

The mounting political instability that followed Trump step by step on the campaign trail continued into November. At a rally on November 3, this time Trump threatened journalists in attendance, as he preached to his choir: "I have this piece of glass here. But all we have really over here is the fake news. And to get me, somebody would have to shoot through the fake news. And I don't mind that so much. I don't mind that" (Lewis 2024).

Despite Trump's increasingly aggressive and demented attacks on democracy and anyone who dared to stand up to him, the $277-Million Musk spent to purchase the presidency[2] was enough to install the convicted felon and his new couch-humping toady[3] JD Vance as the nation's second and third most powerful people.

On November 25, Musk's second-in-command threatened to impose massive tariffs on Canada, Mexico, and China if they did not meet his demands. Reuters reported a day later that Trump had posted on his failing social media platform Truth Social: "On January 20th, as one of my many first Executive Orders, I will sign all necessary documents to charge Mexico and Canada a 25% Tariff

---

2 Elon Musk spent $277Million to get Donald Trump elected.

3 As JD Vance was being confirmed as Trump's 2024 running mate on July 15, an outrageous rumour began circulating on X (formerly Twitter) when a user going by the name of @rickrudescalves wrote that they "can't say for sure but [Vance] might be the first vp pick to have admitted in a ny times bestseller to f***ing an inside-out latex glove shoved between two couch cushions (vance, hillbilly elegy, pp. 179-181)." (Ramirez, 2024). As bizarre as this false accusation might be, it was still somehow hilariously believable enough that several news agencies felt the need to fact check the claim.

on ALL products coming into the United States, and its ridiculous Open Borders" (Pitas 2024).

Adding insult to injury, Trump then attempted to humiliate Canadians in a series of posts online, calling Canada the '51st state', and calling the Prime Minister of Canada 'Governor Trudeau', which is the title for state leaders in the U.S.A. "It was a pleasure to have dinner the other night with Governor Justin Trudeau of the Great State of Canada," Trump said in another social media post. "I look forward to seeing the Governor again soon so that we may continue our in depth talks on Tariffs and Trade, the results of which will be truly spectacular for all!" (Tasker 2024).

The following weeks saw the beginning of a ceasefire between Israel and Hezbollah, and the fall of the Syrian capital of Aleppo to opposition forces. Martial law was also declared in South Korea on December 3, when President Yoon Suk Yeol accused his opposition, the Democratic Party, of sympathizing with North Korea. By December 14, Yoon's powers were suspended after a parliamentary vote impeached him for abusing his power and undermining democracy.

As I was preparing to head out the door on my way to artist Arne Roosman's house on the morning of December 21, I noticed yet another inflammatory tweet posted by the man many are now calling the "real U.S. President-elect", Elon Musk (Lemire, 2025). Acknowledging his support for the far-right Alternative for Germany party, Musk tweeted: "Only the AfD can save Germany" (Margaritoff 2024).

Does it worry you that the 'richest' man in the world is freely promoting a far-right political party founded on racist ideologies, openly affiliated with neo-Nazis, in the very country where Adolf Hitler ruthlessly scapegoated, chased down and systematically exterminated some six million Jews?

Well, it sure as hell does me.

As hopelessly sad and infuriating as it is, this is where we were at on that sunny Solstice afternoon in 2024 when I arrived at Arne's place in Coe Hill.

Widening the angle of our lens to get a clearer look at the seismic shifts in our world order since Arne and I started this conversation in December 2019, I can't help but wonder if people are doomed by the willful ignorance of injustice to repeat the deadly errors of our past. In this relatively brief window of time, we have witnessed profound changes in the world that have reshaped the way we see each other and reality, and all these exacerbated by the COVID-19 pandemic.

What began as an isolated health crisis in the dying moments of 2019 in Wuhan, China, rapidly grew into a public health emergency of unimaginable proportions. By the time we put a ribbon on this book project in late December 2024, this global catastrophe had taken more than seven million lives worldwide (World Health Organization 2024). Exposing both the strengths and weaknesses of modern civilization, people across the globe were suddenly required to deal with public health measures such as lockdowns, travel bans, mask and vaccine mandates. The harsh reality of global inequality became painfully apparent as economic paralysis set in. Every time the pandemic put its foot down hard, the formidable depth of inequities and vulnerabilities within both national and global systems were revealed. Using their economic advantage, the world's wealthiest nations quickly secured vaccine doses, while poorer countries scrambled to secure a foothold in a global race for survival that grew more and more competitive by the day.

Perhaps the most unsettling legacy of the COVID-19 pandemic, however, has been the growing number of far-right movements around the world arising in its wake. From Trump's failed insurrection in the U.S. Capitol on January 6, 2021, to the 'Freedom' Convoy's illegal and costly occupation of Canada's national capital, far-right groups have used the fear and uncertainty caused by the pandemic to take control of the most vulnerable, and use them to promote insane, and often racist conspiracy theories. This pointed vomiting of hate has further divided society by fostering a dangerous 'us versus them' mentality.

The public execution of George Floyd by former Minneapolis police officer and convicted murderer Derek Chauvin on May 25, 2020, amplified racial tensions that had been simmering for years in the U.S.A. and growing worse in the wake of the ongoing pandemic. With evidence showing how COVID-19 was disproportionately affecting BIPOC—in particular, Black—communities, this further heightened people's awareness of systemic inequality and the stark disparities in health-care, economic security, and law enforcement.

During the Presidency of Barack Obama, the first Black leader of the "Free World", the Black Lives Matter movement was born in 2013.

> Opal Tometi, Alicia Garza, and Patrisse Cullors tweeted #BlackLivesMatter in the wake of Trayvon Martin's death. The hashtag helped galvanize a movement calling out the racism that has deeply affected the lives and deaths of Black people in America since its founding. The Black Lives Matter movement calls for the reimagination of institutions like policing, housing, education, and health care, with the hope of redressing the harms done to historically marginalized communities and building a more just country for all. –American Civil Liberties Union, 2023.

The murder of George Floyd saw a resurgence in the Black Lives Matter movement. This time, in a different America under a different president, far-right extremists found fertile ground to spread white supremacist and racist conspiracies against Black activists and their allies in a severe cultural backlash.

These backlash extremists share nationalist ideologies, anti-immigrant rhetoric, and a glorification of 'strongman' leadership. At their core, they reflect a yearning for a past that never truly existed. A past where hierarchical patriarchal authority was unquestioned, and society was neatly divided into the 'deserving' and the 'undeserving'. In countries like Hungary, Poland, and Italy, far-right parties have capitalized on the public's anxieties about economic instability, migration, and co-existence with diverse cultures. Meanwhile, in U.S.A., Trump continues to champion the Ku Klux Klan-inspired "America First" agenda, which remains a powerful rallying cry for white supremacist-friendly extremist factions.[4]

What pisses me off most about these snake-oil-sucking natural born losers, and the resurgence of Nazi and far-right extremism in general, is not just the growing number of people who buy into their ideologies, but the way these movements have taken root in the very institutions designed to protect democracy. The events of January 6, 2021, when Trump supporters stormed the U.S. Capitol, highlighted the stark reality that the erosion of democratic institutions is no longer a hypothetical threat but a very clear and present danger with the potential to tear down democracies everywhere.

Arne and I have been on a journey over the last five years exploring his past and its connection to the present. One of the most important takeaways from our discussions is that a government for the people, elected by the people, is an incredibly fragile thing. That is why anti-democratic and ultra-divisive movements like the ones we have been seeing rear their ugly heads over the past decade, tend to thrive in times of crisis.

What has become clear from listening to Arne share his experience of growing up under Hitler's thumb is that these types of movements are not just a passing political phenomenon—they are

---

4   Author Sarah Churchwell aptly described the connection between Donald Trump, the "America First" slogan, and the KKK in her book *Behold, America: The Entangled History of 'America First' and 'the American Dream'* when she stated: "As this story will show, reactionary populism in the United States has historically defined itself against the same enemies–urban elites, immigrants, liberals, progressives and organised labour; and for the same beliefs–evangelical Protestantism, traditional 'family values' and white supremacy. Trump has once again brought Americans face-to-face with a deeply rooted populist conservatism, one that defines itself in opposition to groups of people it constructs as 'alien' or 'un-American'. And that populism is consistently drawn to demagogues and authoritarians."

symptoms of a larger, more troubling shift in political culture that seems to occur during turbulent times. This rise of far-right, fascist movements such as the "Make America Great Again" (MAGA) movement that we are seeing now, is in many ways a throwback to the most evil and regrettable period of the 20th century. Once again, as it did the 1930s when the world was awash with authoritarian regimes born of the economic turmoil and political instability left behind after the First World War, the Unholy Ghost of fascism has arisen from its grave.

'Twas a Sunny Day tells the story of the rise of 'strongman' despotism through the innocent and unbiased eyes of an Un-German child in Hitlerland, surrounded by the preventable atrocities of war, poverty, and racism. By promising 'strong' leadership in crisis, law and order, and a better world for all who follow orders, and hate who they are told to hate, the sociopathic dictators who have driven these democracy-killing machines throughout history have fortunately left us a blueprint outlining their path to power. But this blueprint does nothing to help guide or assist us in building a better world for good people, if we don't take the time to understand the structure it defines.

As a journalist, I've had the privilege of speaking with a wide range of people—activists, politicians, artists, and even a few good God-fearing folks with an authentic love for Jesus—but none of those conversations have been as intimate, candid, or profoundly life-altering as my dialogues with Arne Roosman. Having witnessed so many monumental moments in modern human history, Arne's story and body of work reflect the times he has experienced. They also stand as testament to the resilience of the human spirit in the face of evil and adversity.

'Twas a Sunny Day is Arne's insatiable curiosity, his practical philosophy of non-violence, and his unwavering commitment to cripple any fascist that gets in his way with creatively aimed laughter. Beyond the historical account of life and art and the turbulent times it highlights, this book is a call to action, an opportunity to look within and honestly question what it is that matters to us most and why.

The wisdom Arne imparts throughout the pages to follow are intended to serve as a beacon leading us away from the swiftly approaching storm on the horizon. Now, as we prepare to take on "Project 2025"[5], we again find ourselves doing our best to get by in a world plagued by war, corrupted by greed, and poisoned by social divisions. Standing on this familiar pile of shattered bones, smelling the same stench of rotting flesh that our ancestors choked on, our unprecedentedly informed yet critically oblivious generation is confronted with a choice that is now more urgent than ever. Do we learn from the fatal mistakes of previous generations and move beyond our suicidal tendency to choose war over peace, and the short-term profits of the greedy few over basic fairness? Or, do we carry on with business as usual and continue to shit where we eat?

---

5   Project 2025 "...is a 900-page policy 'wish list', a set of proposals that would expand presidential power and impose an ultra-conservative social vision. During his campaign, Donald Trump repeatedly disavowed Project 2025, after a backlash over some of its more radical ideas. But he has nominated several of its authors to fill key government positions, and many of his initial executive orders closely follow proposals outlined in the document."

"Bauka", *Arne Roosman,* charcoal on paper, 1965.

LIFE IS BUT A DREAM

A brilliant idea with no God insight.
No devil to care.
The cow jumped over the moon, right there in the child's imagination.
Creation does not a creator need.
It is the very thing our fear of the unknown feeds: the God idea.
The empty to be filled as part of our eloquent fantasy.
The classroom is empty, where the pupils can breathe freely.
Enter Gabriel, master of the horn, feeding the imagination.
Introspection carries the horn.
Its soundscape now, by magic, Gabriella, a child no more.
My brush of the present, the time mixed in, and you have a painting.
Filling the universe with sounds, the viewer can barely hear.
A child of war, blinded by the sunny possibilities of humanity.
It's never too late.
With my artistry, I intend to awaken curiosity,
please the intellect, and all light touch.
– Arne Roosman

DECEMBER 21ST, 2024

Walking into Arne Roosman's home on this first day of winter, as always, felt like returning home after an arduous journey with a mouthful of stories worth telling. And no matter where or when we get together, Arne never falls short of having a story to tell. Sitting across from Arne, one must not forget that on the other side of the table is close to 93 years of experience and the wisdom those years offer someone who lives a life full of purpose, adventure, creativity, and wonder. It was seated at his kitchen table, the exact place we found ourselves in on that morning of December 21, 2024, that Arne shared with me his love of life, wife Liina, his daughters Anne and Rebecca, his parents Helle and Axel, and his two brothers and four sisters. It was there where he explained to me the origins of his personal philosophy and passion for art, beauty, nature and the Creative Spirit.

Once a lofty white pine, a contributing member of a healthy forest, Arne's table served as an altar of sorts upon which we sacrificed copious amounts of strong beer, smelly blue cheese, fine whisky, golden champagne, and potent tequila. That table was the forum for our symposia on the unnecessary evils that politics demand we accept; our esteem for public health-care, education, and the merits of democratic socialism; the philosophies arising from the ashes of war and the fruits of the creative labour; and our quest to establish a more peaceful existence.

Year after year and beer after beer, we sat there at his table laughing, and cursing Nazis, fascists, fat cat wannabe dictators, and all who admire such pointless greed and destructive ignorance. This simple but sturdy piece of furniture was the canvas upon which we created something beautiful. It was the primary platform to exchange ideas about the nightmare of the moment, and the eternal potential for a better dream.

"Good morning, Arne!" I shouted as I opened the front door. Taking a few more steps into the living room, I could see that he was on the phone, so I took a seat in the kitchen and waited for him to finish his call.

"Nate! Good to see you," he said as he walked up the ramp from his art studio to join me at the table. "How are you this morning?"

"Good! Great to see you as well. I brought us a few treats," I said, pointing to the box of apple fritters, blue cheese, crackers, and beer I had brought with me.

"Well, well. What do we have here? Look at this," he said, whistling as he picked up the blue cheese. "And it's after noon, so that means the bar is open."

"That works for me," I said, as I cracked open a couple cans of Boneshaker for us. "Well Arne, here's to another Solstice together."

Arne poured the beer. "Here's to today," he said as we clinked glasses.

"So, how is your dream book coming along? Are you still having the wild dreamscapes you were telling me about?"

"Talk about dreams,"[6] Arne said. "I've had some fantastic

---

6   These quotes are recorded passages of conversations with Arne, transcribed.

dreams lately, early in the morning. But today was the most fantastic dream I've had. When I'm sleeping, well, I think I'm sleeping, and suddenly this person comes in the door, and I think it's a 'he'. I'm not so sure, but they were very tall and had no face. I have a lot of dreams of people, even my relatives, my brother – all the dead people – they're all without heads or their heads are not in focus. They are doing all sorts of things, and I am talking to them, but they never talk back."

"And you can still tell who they all are?"

"Yeah. When I say, 'Look, Benny, why don't you answer me? I just asked you yesterday, blah, blah, blah…', and then when I'm looking at him expecting an answer, his face fades away. Now, he's been dead for 20 years. So, I'm lying there and suddenly this big person comes in with one of your telephones [cellphones]. And do you know what he has on that thing? The portrait of Maria Callas that I drew years ago. And he's showing me this in the dream in the morning. Then I realize, oh shit, it's one of those dreams where I don't get an answer. So, I'm totally conscious now of the dreamscape as I'm experiencing it. Now comes the next phase. So, I'm falling asleep again because I know I want to sleep a little more because the alarm hasn't gone off, and then all of a sudden, the whole dreamscape changes. Next comes the most fascinating thing. Now I'm drifting into an interior that is supreme. All the way up the wall, up to the ceiling, which is made up of little white ceramics. Beautifully done walls, floors, everything is white ceramics. There are about two square inch ceramics everywhere. I'm so fascinated. I know it's a dream, sort of, but I'm so impressed with how beautifully it is done because it goes around every bend. And then suddenly I realize I'm looking at my living room. It is sunny, as bright as it can be and everything is white, crystal white ceramics all over the place. Everywhere I look is this beautiful workmanship and I am so impressed, and I am wondering who the hell did this to my living room."

"It sounds like a work of art … your living room," I said looking around, appreciating the collection of art, photographs, books, and antiques he had thoughtfully arranged to transform his house into an inspiring and welcoming place to call home. "It really is though."

"It hits me that this is all my living room. Only it is wider, and it is all over. It is hovering over you and it's coming at you. It's beautiful. It's like the castle of King Louis the 14th, you know. Just a beautiful piece of classic work. And then suddenly 'Deet! Deet! Deet! Deet! Deet!' I am again awake one minute before my alarm."

"Your body clock is right on time."

"It's amazing these dreams lately, and how much I enjoy them. They're terrific," he said. "I call it conscious dreaming. This is quite recent. Maybe a year ago, I started noticing that I'm consciously dreaming, but now it's almost like every night."

"What a scene, I can picture it. Have you ever thought of painting or drawing your dreams? I recall reading a conversation in Rolling Stone magazine between William S. Burroughs and David Bowie where they were talking about keeping a journal or a tape recorder beside the bed, to try and tap into the creative ideas in their dreams as soon as they woke up."

"Ho, ho. That's too much like Nabokov," Arne laughed.

"Let's eat this mouldy shit," I said, cutting into the wedge of blue cheese I had picked up on the way.

"Delicious," Arne said, biting into a cracker full.

"How has it been keeping up with the world during the postal strike? You must have a pile of magazines and newspapers waiting to be read."

"Not too bad, a few people have brought me newspapers and I have been following on the radio. But there is a lot of nonsense, too many advertisements on the radio. I have my books, so I've been reading and rereading a lot of what's on the shelf."

"Nice. Your library is incredible," I said. "The news is so depressing these days. So much war and racist anti-immigrant garbage. A lot of media bowing to their two daddies, Musk and Trump."

"There is nothing left there [in the U.S.A.] at this stage of the game with their government," Arne said. "We don't have a democratic institution there. It has nothing to do with democracy anymore. It is just a couple of guys doing their thing."

"It's an oligarchy of conmen," I chirped.

"Conmen. That's exactly what they are," Arne fired back. "And this whole 'Trumpian' ideology isn't just going to fade away. Not when we have these assholes like Musk interfering with governments all over the bloody place."

"Did you hear about Trump and Musk's latest horse shit about Canada being the 51st state?"

"Yeah. And they're not joking. This guy is actually serious about it. Deep down, we all know he would love to see that he was the one that brought Canada to the U.S."

"It would be a historic takeover, and it would be in the favour of the U.S., that's for sure. These billionaire types aren't fans of public healthcare or education. If they took those public services away from us there's a shitload of tax dollars there, ripe for the picking."

"This whole thing about Canada becoming the 51st state is almost impossible. But he can play all sorts of games... The people that the system depends on are also so heavily into this money thing that they can't really tell Trump to get lost or say no. They have no option but to go along with it."

"His entire cabinet is made up of billionaires," I said. "These are the guys that are going to, as he says, 'drain the swamp?' Who are they going to serve, the people?"

"Themselves," replied Arne.

"Here's to these greedy bastards and the wool they have pulled over so many working-class people's heads," I said, raising my glass.

"And to all their trillions and zillions of dollars!" Arne added enthusiastically, as we smashed our mugs together, causing our beer to foam up and soak the pile of papers on the table.

"Conmen! And you know for guys like Musk and Trump to get where they are now it took a hell of a lot of conning."

"Definitely," I agreed. "You don't become the richest man in the world without fleecing more than a few folks. I guess that's the nature of capitalism though; when it comes down to it, you are obligated to profit off of someone else's hard work."

"We were worrying about the Conservative Party in Canada—blah, blah, blah, this and that—but the fact is that while we were focused on the same old thing, these cons have taken over the United States. Now we have this oligarchy in charge of one of the biggest political entities and militaries in the world, and Trump keeps on repeating this stupid kind of 'ha, ha, ha' shit joke about us being the 51st state? I don't know, Nate, maybe Canada has had it. Maybe there is no more Canada."

A PEACEFUL PLACE

It is just before midnight on Friday, May 10, 2024, and I am sitting underneath one of two massive white spruce trees beside my home, looking up at the night sky. From somewhere in the darkness of the forest surrounding me, a pair of barred owls is calling out in search of affection. Echoing in all directions, a seasonal serenade rises from the vibrating bellies and throats of a recently awakened choir of spring peepers, endemic to the wetland at the bottom of the hill. It is that time of year again, when Nature's fullness grows with every sunrise.

Fifteen minutes ago, I was inside on the sofa, watching the evening news. My plans for a comfortable evening of writing were disrupted when during the weather report, I discovered that outside, the first G5 solar storm since 2003 was unleashing its hot fire on the solar system. Such storms have been known to cause total blackouts and power grid collapses. On March 13, 1989, for instance, a powerful geomagnetic storm knocked out the Hydro-Québec power grid, leaving some six million people in the dark for nine hours. Another byproduct of this type of cosmic event—also the reason why I traded the comforts of my living room for a seat on the forest floor—was a high probability of witnessing one of Earth's most awe-inspiring spectacles, the Northern Lights.

As I sat there listening to the peaceful noises of Nature at night, my eyes adjusted to the absence of light, revealing to me the cosmic magnificence of the dancing lights, colourfully illuminating the sky above. Pulsing waves of electrons colliding with and energizing different types of molecules, which, once aroused by the interaction, become excited and radiate a rainbow of light.

Soaking in the beauty of the moment, I thought of my friend, the Estonian-born artist Arne Roosman, and how he had told me about observing the *aurora borealis* over Stockholm in the 1950s.

It has been four and a half years since I first took a seat across from Arne at the kitchen table in Coe Hill, where he opened up to me about his extraordinary life story. While the content of these pages includes many of the words and sentiments expressed during our exchanges within this window of time beginning in September of 2019, any information collected for this book in the first two years or so resulted from times I interviewed Arne for the Bancroft newspapers regarding his art. It was while transcribing these conversations that it occurred to me how immensely important it is to share Arne's story now, as the evil forces of fascism attempt to dominate us again.

What caused me to take pause looking at his story, was the recording from December 21, 2019. Four hours, 20 minutes and 32 seconds. Usually, the only time a journalist is tasked with transcribing a recording this long is when covering a protest, a meeting of government officials, or a professional conference, where there are many key players contributing to the conversation. When covering such assignments where truth and the spirit of the situation under the microscope can spontaneously show themselves at any given moment, I have learned that the best strategy is to use the recorder as a sort of trawl net. Getting my feet wet as a full-time reporter for *Bancroft This Week* newspaper back in 2013, I discovered it was much easier to head into these kinds of events with the 'tape' already rolling. Challenging as this is when going over the recording afterwards, casting a wide net simply catches more fish.

It wasn't just the amount of time that caught my attention with this recording from that day in December of 2019. It was also the fact that within the first 20 minutes of our conversation, Arne provided me with all the information I needed to put together an article of at least 1,000 words. Because the weekly Monday and Tuesday morning deadlines always tend to turn up sooner than I would like, I have learned to be strict with my time and not stay longer than necessary to get the information I need to accurately convey a story. As I was re-listening to our discussion almost two years after it took place, it dawned on me that the real story in need of being told was in the labyrinth of unanswered questions springing up from the last four hours of the recording.

I revisited the recording following a conversation with Arne on September 16, 2021. I had dropped by his place that afternoon to photograph some new paintings he had finished as part of his "Filly and Trooper" cartoon series that we were publishing in The Bancroft Times. Again, an assignment that could have been completed in about 20-30 minutes became a three hour and 45-minute dive into his past which planted the seeds that grew into questions and eventually this book.

Nevertheless, it's now almost 3 a.m., and I have been sitting under this tree, admiring the celestial waltz of the Northern Lights for nearly three hours. Mingling in the north, from horizon to Heaven there is a shifting sea of violet, green, blue, and crimson lights. For Swedish fishermen, seeing the aurora borealis was a sign of good fortune. The Sami people of Sweden, Finland, Russia, and Norway believe the Northern Lights are the spirits of their Ancestors communicating with them. Like many other Indigenous cultures around the world, they also see the lights as a good omen with the power to heal and protect people.

No matter which country, religion, or culture one comes from, staring into the *aurora borealis* is a spiritual experience. I should be inside sleeping, but as long as these lights keep dancing, I will remain drawn in by their magnetic pull.

Comfortably resting my back against the tree, I settled in for the whole show. The universe above was shining bright like an emerald in the sun. A piece of the same puzzle, I sat there with my back to the bark, thinking about the day behind me. I spent most of it at Arne's place celebrating Christmas and his birthday. While the Christmas season and Arne's birthday on March 6 were still more than seven months away, his daughter Rebecca and son-in-law Neil were visiting from Edinburgh, Scotland, so he made it an evening to remember. Arne, as he had made it a custom with such festive occasions, ordered a bottle of Armand de Brignac Ace of Spades for us to pay homage to the day and what matters most. With so many reasons to raise a glass that afternoon, he also procured a large goose, which Rebecca prepared along with a variety of roasted vegetables.

Over the years, Arne and I have celebrated: five Christmases; five New Year's'; five Estonian Independence Days; five birthdays; five Easters; four Thanksgivings; and four Halloweens. For Arne, a celebration is always much more than just an opportunity to eat fine foods and drink good booze. For him, every holiday or special occasion is a sacred event worthy of ancient rituals and a festive environment.

First, there must be music; not just any music, but music that suits whatever we are celebrating, and whomever we are celebrating with. The aesthetics of the space in which we recognized days and events as special also played a significant role in defining them as sacred. There were always flowers, candles, and handmade seasonal decorations thoughtfully placed throughout his home.

On this evening, before dinner was served, I, as the designated 'official un-corker of the bottle', emptied the champagne into four glasses.

"To Life!" Arne said, lifting his glass.

"To Life," the three of us responded, clinking our glasses together with his.

As we sat there at Arne's kitchen table, enjoying the food, company, music, and atmosphere, a profound feeling of familiarity came over me. For a couple years I had come to know Rebecca and Neil through my conversations with Arne. Although Rebecca and I had met during one of her previous visits, the four of us being together in the flesh, at the same place and time, was a privilege we had yet to experience.

Rebecca and Neil told us about their lives in Scotland, and day trips from Edinburgh to Glasgow for a dose of its thriving art scene. Arne and I took turns sharing our experiences of living in North Hastings, Ontario. We talked about politics in the U.K., Europe, the U.S.A., and Canada, acknowledging the growing number of politicians worldwide who are embracing anti-Democratic, ultra-nationalist and racist ideologies popular with far-right extremists and white supremacists. We quipped at how someone like The Donald could still be considered a "serious" political contender for the U.S. presidency after all his outrageous lies and crimes. We discussed Greek and Roman mythology, and Rebecca told us about her recently completed Master's thesis on the subject, which Arne and I paid tribute to over another bottle of champagne last fall.

Taking care to be fully present during dinner, I looked around the room as if viewing it with a new set of eyes, to appreciate the unique richness of the scene. Although it was the same room where Arne and I spent hundreds of hours talking, drinking, listening to music, laughing, crying, and sharing stories, I suddenly felt a deeper sense of comfort and connection with the space. It was at this same moment I recognized that each of the dozens of faces staring back at us from the photographs, paintings, and drawings decorating Arne's walls and shelves were those of the people he introduced to me when telling me about his life and art. Present at the party on the wall to my left were Arne's Mother Helle and Father Axel. On the bookshelves behind me, his daughter Anne, Uncle Gustaf, Grandpa Josef Boesberg, and Uku, his beloved furry friend whom I met at his home on the York River in Bancroft when we first crossed paths in 2014.

Of all the eyes looking back at us, there was one pair which stood out among the rest... those being the enchantingly beautiful eyes of Arne's wife Liina. On the shelf to the right of where we were seated and where he almost always sat, there was a photo of Liina propped up against the wall. On that wall there was a portrait he had painted of Liina decades earlier. Above the phone in the studio, there was another photo of Liina. Beside his bed, a large, beautifully framed black and white photograph of Liina. On my way out the door later that evening, I noticed that everywhere I looked, there was Liina.

The magic of Arne and Liina's love story is undeniable. From their brief acquaintance in the Oxford DP camp near Lübeck, Germany after the war, to their chance reunion in Toronto on New Year's Eve in 1957, to the birth of their daughters Anne and Rebecca, and Liina's death on January 1, 2016, whenever Arne spoke of their love or his family, I saw a different side of the man I had come to know through his art, as a friend, a brother, a teacher, and an inspiration. Whenever Liina came up during our conversations I got to know Arne the boyfriend, husband, lover, and father of their children. Anytime Rebecca or Anne popped up in one of our discussions, I had a chance to meet Arne, the proud and loving Dad.

Looking back on that sunny day in December of 2019, we began this conversation unaware that the entire world as we knew it was about to be fundamentally transformed over the next four and a half years. And the biggest agent of change did not waste time getting the ball rolling in 2020. Beginning its reign over the headlines, and everyone on the planet's lives for the next two years, COVID-19 showed up in the U.S.A. on January 20, 2020. Five days later, Toronto reported the first confirmed case in Canada. Within less than two months, the World Health Organization officially declared COVID-19 a global pandemic. At this time 118,000 cases had been confirmed in 114 countries along with 4,291 deaths. From the inaugural traces of the virus that appeared in a wet market in Wuhan City, China back in December of 2019 until summer 2024, these grim global tallies have climbed to 7,050,691 deaths and

775,583,309 confirmed cases. But COVID-19 was just one of many paradigm-shifting events that have taken place in the last four and a half years.

It was amid a rising wave of fear and confusion during the early days of the pandemic that Arne helped to re-inspire my love of print journalism with a generous weekly dose of much needed data. Being an avid reader with a curious mind, Arne has subscriptions to several newspapers and magazines, including: *The New Yorker*, his favourite, *Harpers*, *The London Review*, *MacLean's*, *Architectural Digest*, *TIME*, and *The Walrus*, to name a few. Arne recognized how much I enjoyed reading and discussing the world events stewing in both of our minds and began leaving a dozen or so magazines and newspapers in a special basket to the left of the front door. Taking them home, between each of our visits I would study what he gave me, almost as if I was cramming for a university exam. This weekly dose of facts he presented to me each time we got together not only enhanced my ability to cover the pandemic, it also provided me with a broader frame of context for every other major global event that has happened since.

As I read through the information he gave me after each visit, I discovered marks throughout each of the publications, highlighting quotes and statistics related to our previous discussions. Often his annotations pointed to issues of concern that had yet to reach the mainstream media's radar, but would soon dominate the national, and global conversation. To this day, these magazines, especially those Arne has improved, continue to serve as a valuable resource.

"Ant drawn by Arne in 1939", *Arne Roosman* in *"Touch of Arsenic"*, pencil on paper, 2014.

"Mother, don't cry.", *Arne Roosman,* conte and charcoal on paper, 2019.

In writing this book, they have provided context to Arne's story; transforming it from a basic memoir into a portrait of the artist's philosophy, and how his experience as a lifelong foreigner has shaped him into the man he is today.

A survivor of the bloodlands during the Second World War and a passionate advocate for peace, Arne has never cowered when confronted by tyranny. Rather than bend the knee or turn a blind eye, he has learned to fight back using his art and satire to unveil the corrupted spirits of wannabe dictators, and all those who believe that violence and killing is a better path to power than peace and cooperation. Violence and killing versus peace and cooperation; seems like a no-brainer, but as any student of history will tell you, we as a species have been struggling to choose a side since we invented the idea of war.

That was the critical mistake Hitler made in his 13-year run at a 1,000-year Reich. From the get-go, it was always about "his" struggle, not *unser kampf*. Inevitably this will be the fatal flaw of the American Republican Party. In 2024, their entire existence hinges on the fate of a completely self-absorbed 78-year-old convicted felon, a rapist and a con man who lies as easily as he farts, and will do anything he can to take back the White House.

While working on this project we have witnessed a rise in racial violence and hate crimes around the globe. On February 19, 2020, 11 people were killed and five injured by a far-right extremist near Frankfurt, Germany who went on a shooting rampage at a shisha bar in Hanau. The world changed again just three months later, when the Black Lives Matter Movement garnered international attention as some 15 to 26 million people participated in the protests that followed the public execution of George Floyd – an unarmed Black man who was suspected of using a counterfeit $20 bill to purchase something – by a white police officer in Minneapolis, Minnesota.

Later that year on November 3, 2020, Joe Biden was elected as the 46th President of the United States. Believing Trump's lies that the election had been stolen, his supporters followed their leader's orders and stormed the U.S. Capitol Building on January 6, 2021. The MAGA revolution fell short when upon breaching the building's defences, the insurrectionists resorted to smearing their own feces on the walls and taking selfies while ransacking the desks of their least favourite politicians.

The extreme heat wave impacting Northern California, Idaho, Oregon, Western Nevada, and Washington state in the U.S.A. hit Canada next, creating the perfect conditions for wildfires that would consume forests in British Columbia, Alberta, the Northwest

Territories, Saskatchewan, Manitoba, and Yukon Territory as well. Stretching out over hundreds of square kilometres, the fires that began on June 30, 2021, reduced Lytton, B.C. to ash by July 3. Killing two in Lytton, the heat wave ended the lives of 600 people on the west coast. Twenty-four hours before the fires, Lytton set a record for the hottest temperature ever recorded in Canada at 49.6 °C (121.3 °F).

September 2021, Canadians re-elected Prime Minister Justin Trudeau and the Liberal Party for a third term, only this time with a minority government in need of propping up by the New Democrats. The year 2022 brought us the Canadian version of Trump's January 6 insurrection that came to be known as the "Freedom Convoy".

While Tropical Storm Ana was busy killing 115 people in Madagascar, Malawi, and Mozambique in January 2022, Russian President Vladimir Putin was reviewing his plan to invade Ukraine. On February 24, 2022 – Estonian Independence Day – Putin followed through with his plan to strike Kyiv with missiles before breakfast. In May 2022, 19 students and two teachers were gunned down in a mass shooting at Robb Elementary School in Uvalde, Texas. Altering the political landscape worldwide, Queen Elizabeth II passed away at the age of 96 on September 8, 2022, just seven months after celebrating her Platinum Jubilee, which marked 70 years on the throne in the United Kingdom. To round out another kick in the nuts of a year, a massive winter storm hit southern Canada and the northern U.S.A. December 21 to 26, killing 91 people.

When I went to see Arne on New Year's Day in 2023, there was an unexpected tone of sadness in his voice that I could detect as soon as he said hello. Tragically, he told me that he had recently received word that his daughter Anne had passed away over the holidays. On the table before him was a white candle burning in front of a photo of Anne with a poem written by a friend.

In the tribute to his daughter, Arne had hand-written the excerpt:

"I'm an exceptional girl,
tick tock, tick tock.
Trapped in a prison of
The cruel design of the
Invisible Hand,
tick tock, tick tock.
Won't you take me out to play?
You'll never make music as
good as this."[7]

"Helle", *Arne Roosman*, charcoal on paper, 1970.

---

7   The excerpt is a passage from Cameron Dreamshare's novel, "Valkyrie's Adonis: A World So Small".

I dropped by Arne's place to celebrate his 91st birthday with him on March 6, 2023. Proudly, Arne shares his birth date with several artists and writers that he admires, and whom he toasts at every one of his birthday parties. A few notable creatives sharing the date with Arne include the Italian sculptor, painter, architect and poet of the High Renaissance from Caprese, Tuscany, Michelangelo in 1475; the French novelist and playwright, Cyrano de Bergerac in the year 1619; and, the Viennese composer, Oscar Straus in 1870.

The party would not last long in 2023. From late spring until Autumn, the climate crisis became a part of our daily lives in a more intrusive manner than we had previously experienced, when the hottest year on record scorched the Earth, sparking a deadly record-breaking wildfire season. In early August the unnaturally high temperatures on land throughout 2023 also caused the world's oceans to reach a new record high temperature of 20.96°C (69.73°F), breaking the previous record in 2016. Less than a week after the National Oceanic and Atmospheric Administration acknowledged the "grim implications" of these numbers for the planet and all who reside here, wildfires ravaged the Hawaiian island of Maui, killing 101 people.

Every time we tune into the news nowadays it appears as if we are on the cusp of a global societal collapse. As a result of more than three decades of inaction on the climate crisis, the catastrophic consequences of leaving anthropogenic global heating virtually unchecked, have become all too tangible and unavoidable. There is something to be said about the fact that in all of Arne's 92+ years on this planet, he has never witnessed wildfire smoke filling lungs across Canada, let alone cross the Atlantic Ocean and blanket European countries such as Portugal and Spain.

The world changed again on October 7, 2023 when Hamas carried out a day of rage inside Israel, killing 1,139 people. Since then, Israel has waged a genocidal campaign of revenge on the Palestinian people that has seen more than 37,000 killed – nearly half of which have been children – with the death toll rising every day.

The day's first light has arrived and is dissolving the majesty of the Northern Lights. One very memorable day is coming to an end, as another begins. Almost five hours I have been sitting here in the dirt and the spruce cones, reflecting on the day and the past four and a half years. The aurora borealis has disappeared but the owls are still talking. Living here in the woods over the past 17+ years, I've learned to pay attention to owls. As lore from many cultures around the world suggests, when owls make their presence known, there tend to be big changes afoot.

I watched the sunrise and then went inside to make a pot of coffee and type up what I had put down on paper overnight. There is still a ton of work to be done before this beast is ready to be unleashed on the press, however, I can finally see the big picture that we have been assembling in these pages at Arne's kitchen table, in roadside pubs, moving cars, hospital waiting rooms and doctors' offices. When Arne and I set out on our journey through the past, I initially imagined this book as a sort of memoir. Now that we are nearing the end of the assembly process, I can see that it has evolved into something with a wider scope.

Studying Arne's artwork in *Touching the Great Again: Visiting a Nursery*, along with my writing leading up to this book, both of us could see the irreversible damage to democracy that Trump's first term was causing. We were also both aware of how dangerous it would be to give this greed-worshipping goon another chance to ruin the "Free World" for another four more years.

At the root, it has been our concern for democracy motivating us to share Arne's story. As a child growing up within Hitler's Reich, and then coming of age while living in DP camps in post-war Germany, Arne's firsthand experience of the Second World War provides a unique perspective on a transformational and dark period of human history. With the MAGA movement threatening a civil war if their Messiah does not win, Arne's observations of what life was like for a young un-German with open eyes and receptive ears living under a racist, tyrannical cult leader, whose followers were willing to eliminate anyone with different political views than their own, could not be more timely.

Spending time with Arne is always an enlightening experience. A master of his passions and the skills they require, whether speaking with his words, a pencil, or a paintbrush, he is a professional planter of seeds that grow into food for thought. From the trail of clues he leaves for me in the basket of magazines by the door, to the stories he tells, Arne lives, creates, and communicates with meaning. He does not waste time on the sleazy sales pitches of known purveyors of lies and misinformation; therefore, when one comes knocking, he can smell their putrid scent from a mile away.

Living in an age when it has somehow become acceptable for our elected officials to blatantly lie and embrace so-called "alternative facts", Arne has no good reason to stay silent about their deliberate deceptions. Seeing the many parallels between the cruel and divisive white nationalist philosophy of the Nazis he grew up with, and the fascist ideologies of the racist clown brigade attempting to revive the far-right today, Arne never shies away from telling it like it is.

The no-holds-barred honesty of Arne's observations and interpretations of a divided world at war and on the brink of societal collapse — a description which is fitting our world today too much like the one that forced a young Roosman family to trade their family home in Estonia for more cramped quarters inside Nazi Germany — delivers us fresh insight into our ongoing fight against those who prefer deranged dictators to democratically elected leaders. Whenever I come away from a conversation about his experiences during the war and the state of global politics today, I am reminded that the American writer Mark Twain was on point in 1874, when he wrote, "History never repeats itself, but the Kaleidoscopic combinations of the pictured present often seem to be constructed out of the broken fragments of antique legends" (Twain 1874).

Democracy vs. Fascism

Democracy

1. Of the people, for the people and by the people.
2. Peasant class given first consideration always.
3. Manufacture, distribution and exchange of goods to suit human needs.
4. Loans and credits by National Bank.
5. Crop insurance.
6. Co-operative business.
7. No exception by Big Business.
8. Free education and health service.
9. Full employment. No relief.
10. Good roads and rural Hydro.
11. Freedom of speech, assembly and Industry.
12. Pensions revised--old age at 60.

Fascism

1. Bureaucratic control. (2% of Canadians control the other 98%.
2. Politicans and High Class first.
3. Manufacture, distribution and exchange of goods for personal profit only.
4. High interest. No credit unions.
5. Farmers removed from farms by mortgage holders.
6. Big Business dictates prices and practices.
7. Those who can, must pay; the rest do without.
8. Relief, Dole, Bread Lines.
9. Gestapo tatics on all citizens not in Government clique.
10. Might is right.
11. Other political parties "not permitted."

Which Will You Have? Democracy! Of Course!

Vote C. C. F.

Vote TURNER

MEETINGS

Actionlite, June 2   Cordova, June 5   Cooper, June 6   Norwood, June 7
Warsaw, June 8
Coe Hill, June 9   Dr. Lorna Thomas.

Ralph Turner, Federal Candidate

HASTINGS-PETERBORO C. C. F. ASSOCIATION

WAY OF LIFE...

"Democracy vs Fascism" Political Ad. *The Bancroft Times*. May 31, 1945.

On several occasions, Arne and I pondered the frightening possibility of another four years of white nationalists and fascists running rampant throughout the United States and Canada, pretending that they are making North America and eventually the world, "great again."

Great? America? Canada? Again? Considering our ancestors' brutal assault on Turtle Island and the Indigenous peoples who have served as stewards of the land, air, and water since time immemorial, it is fair to question when, if ever, America or Canada was truly great.

Something my time with Arne has taught me is that there never really was a "good old days." Every step forward has come at a cost. Is it even possible for nations that were founded on genocide, and empowered by slavery and colonization to achieve greatness? Optimistically, I would like to say yes, because if I am wrong, there is simply no hope for humanity. Most modern cultures and countries have attained status in the world through one form of injustice or another. Over a relatively short period of time, we humans have become well-versed in establishing power through killing, and our individual acceptance of lethal collateral damage in the name of "progress." Nonetheless, as unacceptable as humanity's atrocities are, they are byproducts of who we are and where we came from. As comforting as it would be to wipe our collective conscience clean and begin anew, the crimes of our ancestors must not be cancelled. They exist in our consciousness as useful wisdom, opportunities to evolve and improve our chance of collective survival.

The strength and adaptability of the refugee Roosman family amid such a hostile world speaks volumes to our species' will to survive. When the fighting stopped and the final scores were scratched into the history books, 75 million people had lost their lives because of the war. Seventy-five million people were gone, wiped from the face of the Earth within less than six years, leaving behind—as war inevitably always does—a population contaminated by hate and trauma.

In life, all any of us truly want is peace. I believe this to be a true statement for all living beings, human or non-human. This is why dogs, like cats, horses or even pigs for that matter, prefer to be rubbed opposed to being kicked. Despite our knowledge of this most basic desire at the root of all intention, too many today still choose to conveniently ignore the suffering of refugees fleeing their homeland to seek sanctuary from violence, or build a better, healthier and happier life. Like the Roosmans, they too desire and deserve a peaceful place to call home.

Turning on the evening news, now when I see the faces of displaced people living in refugee camps, I think of the Roosmans. When I see the children in these camps playing in the street with empty water bottles or whatever they can get their hands on, I am reminded of Arne, and how his war-torn childhood ensured that he would never take peace for granted.

Falling asleep with the sun shining through the window on my face, I thought of all the events that persuaded Arne to cross the Atlantic so long ago. Watching the birds hop from branch to branch on the cedar tree in my front yard, it dawned on me that at the root of Arne's immigration journey was his yearning for a peaceful place where he could be free to create. Enjoying the serene vision outside my window, I drifted into dreamland appreciating a peaceful sense of harmony with the forest I call home.

When I awoke from my slumber staring upward through the branches of the cedar tree outside of my window, I realized that the best way to fully appreciate Arne's story is by first finding one's own peaceful place. Only then, after taking the time to understand how vital this place in which peace exists is to our health and happiness can we begin to imagine what life is like when that peace evaporates.

"A Peaceful Place", *Arne Roosman,* charcoal on paper, 2019.

Before reading any further, take a moment to close your eyes and imagine your own peaceful place. Now, with this place in mind, ask yourself these following questions:

What does it look, sound, feel, and smell like?

Where are you?

Who are you with?

What are you doing?

Why are you doing it?

How do you feel?

Do you want to fight? Kill? Destroy?

Why would you?

"Up there, stupid!", *Arne Roosman,* conte, charcoal, and coloured pencils on paper, 2022.

He who cannot obey himself will be commanded.
That is the nature of living creatures.
— Friedrich Nietzsche, 1883–1885

TOUCHING THE GREAT AGAIN

There I was, standing on the corner of Wollaston Lake Road in Coe Hill, waiting for a ride that I wasn't sure was coming. It was December 21, 2019 – the Winter Solstice – a sacred day for many people and cultures around the world. The sun was still shining, but it was just after 4 p.m. and the day's light was beginning to disappear. There were flurries floating on the cold breeze coming in from the north, slowly riding gravity to their seasonal destination.

I spent most of the day at Arne's place just down the road. We had decided to get together that day after reconnecting a few months earlier in September for an interview regarding A Touch of Jazz – an exhibition opening he had coming up a month later at Studio Dreamshare in Pembroke. It was during our conversation about the show that I started to notice our friendly working relationship was evolving into a very real and deep friendship.

Our interview on that day in December of 2019–as with most of our engagements over the years–turned out to be a visit that lasted almost four and a half hours, six beers, and half a bottle of Irish cream whisky. Chewing the fat, we discovered our shared love of music, especially jazz and classical, Ella Fitzgerald, Nat King Cole, Natalie Cole, Oscar Peterson, Beethoven, and Schubert. We spoke of the healing power of art; the disappearing art of philosophy; our reverence for beauty; the absurdity of U.S. president Donald Trump's infantile behaviour, and the innate ugliness of his neo-fascist "MAGA" movement. Strange as it may sound, when I look back on this time, in a way, I feel a sense of gratitude to the one they call "The Donald" for his role in bringing Arne and I together and inspiring this philosophical exchange.

The sun was now gone, and the longest night of 2019 had just begun. The lack of response from the taxi company to the message I left on their machine when I left Arne's place meant that I was likely in for a very long, cold walk home. Calling again and leaving another message, I decided to start walking along Hwy 620 towards my home in L'Amable. Making my way north on the dark highway, I could feel the cold wind penetrating the openings in my clothing and burning my skin. To take my mind off the frigid predicament, I thought about my visit with Arne and the new project that he had been working on. In an attempt to enhance my distraction, I hit play on my voice recorder and listened to our conversation from earlier that day.

"Arne! How are you doing this morning?" I yelled, peeking my head in the open doorway between the front entrance mudroom and his living room.
"Hello! Who is there?" he yelled back from the studio space off the kitchen.
"It's me, Nate. I brought coffee and apple fritters."
"Nate! Come on in and have a seat. I'll be right there."
Walking through his home that morning it felt as if I was entering a ceremonial space. On the kitchen table there were several candles, carefully placed around a wood carving of an evergreen tree that he had decorated with white lights, red bows, and silver tinsel. On the radio, there was classical Christmas music playing loudly. I sat down at the table, soaking in the unique ambience of the room as he made his way up the ramp to join me.
"Thanks for the goodies."
"No problem. I brought us some cream for the coffee, Irish cream," I said, pulling the 'twenty-sixer' out of my backpack.
"Aha! Whisky."
"Well, it is the most wonderful time of the year," I said, pouring a couple shots into each of the mugs Arne had set up in

anticipation of our visit.

"At least that's what the song on the radio is saying," Arne chuckled. "To life!" he said as he raised his cup. "What a nice surprise. Thank you."

"You're very welcome. It's always nice to see you and catch up. Plus, it's the holidays so we have to celebrate."

"There's always a reason to celebrate," Arne said. "That's the secret."

"It looks like you've been a busy man," I said, motioning to the traces of creativity throughout the room. "Are you working on something new?"

"This is what I've been up to," Arne said with a smile, as he pushed a big red binder across the table.

Loosely organized into the book were a stack of roughly two dozen sketches along with several notes, loosely attached to the drawings with green masking tape and staples. On the cover of the binder in gold ink were the words, *Touching the Great Again: Visiting a Nursery.*

I carefully flipped through the pages in an effort not to disturb their order. With each turn I followed his orange-haired, dirty-diaper-waving wannabe dictator on the road to ruin. Stapled to one of Arne's drawings of the infantile ruler, fast asleep on a bed of coins and cash — was a quote:

> *How does tyranny arise? That it comes out of democracy is fairly clear. Does the change take place in the same sort of way as the change from oligarchy to democracy? Oligarchy was established by men with a certain aim in life: the good they sought was wealth, and it was the insatiable appetite for money-making to the neglect of everything else that proved its undoing. Is democracy likewise ruined by greed for what it conceives to be the supreme good?*
> — **Plato's** *The Republic*

As was its intention, the quote that Arne had chosen caused me to question: *From where does tyranny arise? Can a democracy function as long as greed remains unchecked? Do most people need a leader to tell them what to do and who to hate? Was Nietzsche right? Do we earn our freedom by taking control of ourselves?* These were all questions that had been on my mind regularly since The Donald seized the White House in 2016.

"People like these so-called 'strong men', as they are called... 'strong men'," Arne said, raising his fist. "I've heard Trump referred to as one of these 'strong men'; and how it is part of his 'appeal' as the media says. When I hear that I wonder what they mean by strength, and what it means to be a 'strong man'. Does being a 'strong man' just mean being a greedy, racist asshole and a bully? If you ask Dr. Freud or Dr. Jung, the 'strong man' is probably a weak man trying to hide his weakness."

"That sounds about right. There are definitely more than a few insecurities they are over-compensating for. At least a few intellectual deficiencies as well."

I could hear myself pour another splash of Irish cream into my coffee on the tape as I told Arne about the time I drove south to Washington, D.C. to cover the March for Science for Toronto's Now magazine in 2017. I explained to him how before I set out on the nearly 10-hour trek south to D.C., I had the chance to interview a psychology professor at Brock University, named Dr. Tony Volk.

I recounted the interview for Arne, and how even then, Volk could sense the potentially catastrophic impact of Trump's shitstorm coming. At the time, the professor labeled Trump a "narcissist" who exhibited the same characteristics as most of the dictators that humanity has eliminated in the past. One of the most dangerous things about this type of individual, Volk explained to me, was that if they don't like the truth, they will simply make up a "reality" that works for them. When it comes to Trump and others who fit the same profile, I recounted to Arne, how Volk told me that he is the kind of person who will do whatever he wants, no matter the cost to others.

Little Bird Say "It Small"
Caramba - Good Heavens
Carajo - Damn It
Para Que - What For
Es Esto - This Thing
Pequeno - Very Small

"Por encima del muro", *Arne Roosman,* conte, charcoal, and coloured pencils on paper, 2021.

"In other words, it's all about him," I said. "As soon as anyone disagrees with him – even if they are his biggest supporter – they're done, and they're not a part of his club anymore. So many people could see it coming, but somehow, we couldn't stop it... It's disturbing that people admire his illusion of strength so much more than they do people who are genuinely strong."

"A lot of our neighbours never take it that far," Arne responded. "Most people that vote, vote by habit since they are expected to vote. Democracy depends on those that expect to be engaged. Without them we get nowhere. That keeps a lot of people on the sidelines away from action though, because they say, 'Well, it doesn't matter what I say, nobody will listen'. I think that's where we are at now. Even when we elect a good leader, or at least not a horrible leader, they don't really get your attention as much because things are OK. But then, when we get a terrible leader, say a tyrant like Trump, they may be awful, absolutely disgusting in every way, yet there will always be more than enough people who like that terribleness."

"They're passionate about Trump because he gives them permission to hate," I said. "Whether they hate different races, genders – any group of people different than they are really – Trump is there to empower them to hate themselves."

"That's right!" said Arne. "He says exactly what they want to hear to rile them up."

"Are they that bored? I queried. "But I guess when things are good, people don't make as much noise. We're not out in the streets with signs saying, 'Thanks for the roads, schools, and hospitals!' I think most of us here take that stuff for granted, so it's not as exciting as it is for them when Trump says, 'We have to kick the Mexicans and the Muslims out!' He gives us an enemy."

"Crazy, crazy world!" said Arne. "What are we going to do about it, Nate?"

I thanked Arne for the sneak peek at his book, and suggested we get together in the new year to work on a story about the book for the *Bancroft This Week* newspaper. Upon agreeing to meet again in early January, he handed me the binder.

"Take this with you," he said. "You can get acquainted with the story that way. Also, if you don't mind giving it a look with your editor's eye I would appreciate it."

"Sure, I would love to! Cool. Thanks Arne."

"Thank you. Have a Merry Christmas."

"Merry Christmas to you too. I'll see you next year."

"Ho! Ho! Ho! That's right. See you next year."

It was now nearly 7 p.m. and survival was at the front of my mind. I had been walking for more than two hours and my feet felt like they were frozen solid. Although the darkness made it difficult to take in my surroundings, I could tell from the soft glow radiating from the snow-covered surface of the wetland on my left, that I was getting close to the intersection of Hwy 620 and Old Hastings Road.

I walked for about another half hour until I was picked up by a kind dope-smoking, whisky-drinking snowplow driver named Frank. I could tell right away from the curve of his smile in his eyes and the smell of marijuana in the vehicle that he was operating on a higher level. Offering me a chug from his bottle which I happily accepted, he told me about how he was on his way to work at a logging operation near Haliburton for the week. Throughout the next 20 minutes he gave me a detailed account of his job clearing roads through the forest and having to work over the holidays to "pay Santa's bill."

Ever since he was a kid, Frank had always wanted to drive a snowplow. Pushing through the snow and piling it up so that others could get where they were going gave him a feeling of satisfaction, he said.

"It's a good gig," he said, taking another hit off the bottle

"'Tis the Season (Rough Sketch)", *Arne Roosman,* pencil on paper, 2021.

tucked between his seat and the console. "I've been driving these things for over 20 years, so it's like breathing for me now."

"Twenty years, eh! You must know the roads here really well."

"Hell yeah. I can do them with my eyes closed now," he said, shutting his eyes for a few seconds.

"I bet," I said, laughing as he passed me the bottle with his eyes still shut. "I ran auto parts and a bunch of other things over the border in a 20-foot cube van for a few years and I enjoyed being on the road. You learn a lot."

"That's for sure. Especially driving at night. That's why I love plowing," he said. "I put on some Johnny Cash, have a couple drinks, a few puffs, and it's a party, not work. When I was 18, my father told me to find a job that I enjoyed doing and I would never have to work a day in my life. So, I did, and here I am."

Warming my hands over the heating vents, I thought about his father's advice and how my father had told me pretty much the same thing when I was around that age. Before I knew it, we had put a serious dent in the bottle, and Frank was pulling over at the end of my road to drop me off. Thanking him for the ride and for his kindness, I offered him the $20 bill I had in my pocket, but he refused and wished me a Merry Christmas.

"Merry Christmas my friend. Don't work too hard," I said.

"I never do," Frank laughed. "I work smart."

"Safe travels!"

Climbing down from the passenger seat, I closed the door, saluted him goodbye, and made my way home along the Heritage Trail in the dark.

"'Tis the Season", *Arne Roosman*, oil on wood panel, 2021.

"A mouthful of hot air", *Arne Roosman,* conte and ink on paper, 2021.

We are very, very close to being able to ignore Trump most nights....
I truly can't wait ... I hate him passionately ... That's the last four years.
We're all pretending we've got a lot to show for it,
because admitting what a disaster it's been is too tough to digest.
But come on. There isn't really an upside to Trump.
– Tucker Carlson (Bauder & Riccardi 2023)

"Con-Boy/Back to School", *Arne Roosman*, mixed media on paper, 2021.

VISITING A NURSERY

Stepping into the warmth of my home 10 minutes later, I took the red binder out of my backpack and carefully placed it on the dining room table. Eager to dive into Arne's new manifesto, I opened it up. Inside, the pages were populated with a clumsy, dirty diaper-clad, almost likeable obese character, stumbling through the perils of a privileged life. The cartoons poked fun at the former reality TV "star" president turned cult leader, and all those who choose to follow him, by capturing the spirit of the greedy tantrum-throwing toddler tyrant main character, as he cozies up with dictators, fascists, and Nazis. I spent the next week and a half appreciating how Arne's drawings captured the essence of a schoolyard bully's mentality; realizing more and more as I studied his drawings how predictably dangerous someone with that type of mentality can be, when they are given unbridled power.

"Not a drop wasted", *Arne Roosman,* mixed media on paper, 2023.

"Faith-Book", *Arne Roosman,* mixed media on paper, 2021.

"In celebration of the "Good" Kraut", *Arne Roosman,* mixed media on paper, 2021.

A greedy and infantile narcissist,
fulfilling his tyrannical aspirations.
Bored with the limitations of the constitution,
he stumbles through Life,
wasting time and resources while pissing on the people beneath him.

"Riding the Republicans/Up Yours!", *Arne Roosman*,
mixed media on paper, 2021.

Trampling anyone and anything in his path,
he recklessly ruins lives and the planet,
striving at all costs to achieve the same "God-like" status
all aspiring dictators dream of.
Completely oblivious to the insanity he embraces with every breath.

"No Reflection Necessary", *Arne Roosman,* mixed media on paper, 2021.

Standing naked in front of the mirror, he is confronted with his hero, and the words of the French libertarian socialist philosopher Albert Camus:

"Alas, after a certain age, every man is responsible for the face he has."

"Up the 18th", *Arne Roosman,* mixed media on paper, 2021.

Pulling up his diaper,
Donald yells furiously at his limo driver/caddy:
"Take me to the ninth hole!"

It is As Easy As Cheating On Your Income Tax

"It is as easy as cheating on your income taxes or your pregnant wife.", *Arne Roosman*, mixed media on paper, 2021.

"It's as easy as cheating on your income taxes or your pregnant wife," he says, teeing off for the second time on the same hole that day.

NEW YEAR'S DAY 2020

I left home for Arne's place around 10:30 a.m. with plans to celebrate the arrival of 2020 and spend the day reviewing the notes I had made on *Touching the Great Again: Visiting a Nursery*. On my way to Coe Hill, I was overcome with that unexplained feeling of hope for the year ahead that one only experiences on the first day of a new year. The lightly falling snow and bursts of sunshine breaking through the clouds only enhanced this seasonal sentiment further.

Pulling into Arne's driveway just after 11 a.m., Neil Young's song "Old Man" was playing on the radio. There was a White-tailed deer looking in his kitchen window that appeared not to be disturbed at all by my arrival. The snow was beginning to come down a bit heavier now as I sat there admiring its beauty. Grabbing Arne's binder from the passenger seat, I nodded hello to his curious four-legged neighbour and went inside. Taking my boots off in the mud room, I could see through the window in the living room door that Arne was sitting at the kitchen table, petting his friend and most familiar companion, Latte—the striped, orange male cat that he had rescued from a local Animal Hospital in nearby Apsley.

"Come in," Arne shouted in response to my door knocking.
"Good day, Arne, Latte! How are you guys doing today?"
"Great. I got up early to get dressed up for the celebration."
"Looking good, Arne. Happy New Year!"
"Happy New Year. Would you like some coffee?"
"Sure, thanks."

Filling two cups with black coffee, Arne passed me a glass and then offered some of the gingerbread he had made using a recipe his mother Helle picked up in Sweden more than 60 years ago.

Page by page, we turned through the binder, addressing each of the points I had highlighted with my "Editor's eye", as Arne called it. Realizing that we were on the same page in terms of our interpretation of Trump's character and the dangerously toxic nature of the MAGA cult, he explained to me how he had started paying closer attention to U.S. politics since the red hats began waving for Trump during the 2016 presidential campaign.

"There is one thing about history that we all know."

"What's that Arne?"

"We keep quoting about it, but we also ignore it. That is the fact that history is constantly repeating itself."

Having seen nefarious characters like the then U.S. president rise and fall on several occasions throughout his life, Arne told me that he felt a sense of duty to use his art and satire as a sort of tool for chiseling away at the foundation of tyranny. This latest book of art, he said, was a reminder for people today that history is still repeating itself. For Arne, satire has also always been a kind of weapon that he used now and then to hit the destructively corrupt "where it hurts ... their ego," he said. "Satire is very important because you can use it to take these guys and shake them, hurt them, and make them into a painful part of history that we would rather forget. I have scar tissue here and there and that scar tissue reminds me of the pain. But that pain is gone and that's where it should be. Satire is the best kind of medicine for correcting that kind of sentiment that enters, that these tyrants and bad people use to try and glorify themselves. It is like they all want to be a God."

It was at this point in our conversation that Arne first revealed to me that the origin of his disdain for dictators stemmed from his experiences growing up as a refugee in Europe, during and after the Second World War. With relatively little detail – facts that would eventually emerge from hundreds of hours of conversation over the next five plus years – he explained briefly how after the Russians occupied Estonia in 1940, and were rounding up all the Jews, the Roosman family was forced to seek sanctuary in his paternal grandmother's homeland of Germany. Which was then, 300+ years later, under Hitler's control.

Having devoted most of our time to discussing his new book, *Touching the Great Again: Visiting a Nursery*, we did not have time to discuss the nature of these experiences and how they impacted his life. Still, he told me enough to inspire a line of questioning that has yet to find its final answer. Little did we know in the moment we said goodbye that night, that in less than a month, our world was about to go through a sea-change unlike either of us had experienced to date.

"A Lone Wolf", *Arne Roosman,* charcoal and ink on paper, 2014.

The first peace, which is the most important,
is that which comes within the souls of people
when they realize their relationship,
their oneness with the universe, and all its powers;
and, when they realize that at the centre of the universe dwells the Great Spirit,
and that this centre is really everywhere,
it is within each of us.
– Black Elk, 1953

A CHANGE OF PLANS

COVID-19 first put its foot down in Canada on January 25, 2020, when a man tested positive for the virus after returning home to Toronto from Wuhan, Hubei, China. By the time the World Health Organization officially declared COVID-19 a pandemic on March 11th, the total number of confirmed cases worldwide had climbed to more than 182,000. Less than a week after the WHO made the announcement, it was reported that the first case documented in Canada on January 25 had grown to 424 confirmed cases nationwide, with 177 of those cases in Ontario.

With the number of confirmed cases and deaths from the mysterious new virus rising rapidly around the world, the global, national, provincial and local response to the pandemic evolved equally as quickly.

Within hours of the WHO declaring COVID-19 a global pandemic a societal panic set in. Feeling the fear myself, I remember driving straight to the local grocery store with the intention of stocking up for what at the time seemed like the Apocalypse, only to find row upon row of empty shelves. There were no dried or canned beans, no canned vegetables, no bottled water, not a single loaf of bread or bag of flour, and not a roll of toilet paper to be found anywhere. There was also an extremely limited supply of fresh produce, dairy products, and meat. There's nothing like coming face to face with a grocery store with more than half of its shelves empty at 2 p.m. to wake you up to the very real and dangerous fragility of our "grow-it-elsewhere" food system.

The fear and uncertainty caused by the overwhelming abundance of unknowns regarding this unprecedented global public health crisis quickly took its toll on people's mental health. Public health measures meant to protect the spread of the virus, such as masks, temporary lockdowns and non-essential business closures, handwashing, vaccines, etc. were suddenly becoming points of contention for anyone who chose to listen to bleach-injecting boobs, rather than trust the teams of epidemiologists, scientists, and health care professionals who dedicated their lives to protecting and improving public health, long before anyone had even heard of COVID-19.

"Back to work", *Arne Roosman*, mixed media on paper, 2021.

People demand freedom of speech as a compensation for the freedom of thought which they seldom use.
— Søren Kierkegaard, 1843

A TOUCH OF DELUSION

Even a touch of delusion can be a dangerous thing in the mind of someone with more power in their hands than they can honestly handle in good faith. With the fear and uncertainty caused by the pandemic twisting the already twisted, in the spring of 2020 there was a disturbing shift in tone with the Letters to the Editor I was receiving, as the Editor of the two local weekly newspapers in Bancroft. I noticed evidence of the worsening state of the public's mental health in my inbox. The first letter of this type showed up on April 30, 2020. It was a response to an editorial column I had written about our former Conservative MP in Hastings–Lennox and Addington, Derek Sloan and his quest to transform the Tories into the far-right party of his wet dreams, the reader wrote:

> *To the Editor,*
>
> *I was wondering if you are a liberal fascist or simply just ignorant? Look into the coronavirus that mass media and newspapers like yours censor...*
> *You obviously know that only white people can be racist, right? Yes, you and your editorial opinions with zero accountability, nobody else can have opinions, and facts are all conspiracy theories, right. Are you sure you are not a jewmedia publication? or simply liberal fascist? Why don't you sign up for the vaccine, ID2020 and while you are at it, stand in front of the 3g, 4G and the latest 5G microwave towers and transmitters, for at least 5 minutes, but since you don't believe that is harmful, why not an hour or two?*

And don't forget take some toxic anti viral drugs...get connected to a ventilator to get some air and see what it feels like to have your lungs pumped full of air so they burst...and on your way to the retirement homes, put on your dark sunglasses or look the other way, so you don't see the microwave transmitters on top of the wifi everywhere...have some food, drink some water, try talking to your relatives, stay a while...

You are for abortion? Infanticide, euthanasia, child sex trafficking, pedofiles, organ harvesting, alternate sexually degenerate lifestyles, race hating & race treason, race extinction, endless white guilt????
You are for race replacement immigration, no borders?
You are for liberalism of crime, treason, genocide, war and immorality? You know that diversity is a code word for white genocide, good for you!
You are NDP candidate? Did you know that the NDP has their allegiance to the socialist international? This is treason to Canada. The NDP leader has no business in Canada, and he is a member of a separatist extremist group, he is disqualified totally, with his religious above the law credentials...The NDP should not even exist as a party, it is against Canada and is not in accordance with confederation, like everything else. and yes, the NDP lots of sexual misfits, a great homofascist bunch of idiots, good for you, you have lots to be proud of.
This is an editorial opinion, so I can say anything....have a great weekend!
— Subject: 'Re: Boldly Backwards'

There were plenty of others that came in after that "informing" me about the "plandemic", as they so cleverly often called it. However, it was after the Trump-led insurrection on January 6, 2021, that I noticed more and more of the correspondence that I was receiving was taking on a more alarming tone. Another reader stated:

To the Editor,

Can someone at your paper please muzzle that left wing typist in a toque Nate Smelle from spreading anymore propaganda? His articles are so sickeningly left wing in a predominantly center to right wing town that he is an embarrassment to our region.

His latest commentary bashing the so-called riot on Capitol Hill shows what a blind and extremely biased reporter he is. He never once wrote an article chastising the BLM/Antifa riots that did far more harm.

All over the internet there are reams of video, and interviews that contradict the main street media's calculated perversion of what happened at the Capitol.

Not only is Smelle commenting on something way above his pathetic little head, he is dragging American politics into a small peaceful town..inciting his own form of revolution to likely try and justify his pathetic life.

In his article he labels Trump supporters essentially as mindless white supremacists.

Please chastize this kid or move him on, as we can't stomach his commentaries any more.

The Pushback is coming Smelly typist, and the clear idiocy that you smear on the newspaper will be stuck all over your face as the world wakes up. That will be a GREAT DAY! Hopefully, then Bancroft This Week will kick your ass to the curb, and get a real journalist. Maybe you could get a real job like cleaning up all those face diapers, plaguing the environment, that you are so sworn to protect.
— **Subject: 'The Pushback is coming'**

Annoying and disturbing as these personal attacks were, it was a message left on my personal cell phone in the early days of the "Freedom" Convoy's illegal occupation of Ottawa that forced me to do something I had never done before... call the police.

The whining voice on the phone, which was obviously someone trying to disguise who they were, shouted:

"Mr. Smelle! We are so tired of your climate crisis and COVID bullshit! We are coming for you motherfucker!"

The message left me reeling for days. It was not my first death threat as a "small-town journalist." However, because of the pandemic-inspired anxiety and rage running rampant at the time, I took it very seriously. Choosing not to back down, or change a thing about my writing, the letters of the same continued to come in on a regular basis. Many came from anonymous sources or obviously fake names, although there were a few brave idiots who opted to attach their real names.

"I'm a Free Man", Ad in *The Bancroft Times*. October 8, 1942.

"Diapers off", *Arne Roosman,* mixed media
on paper, 2021.

It is difficult to free fools from the chains they revere.
— **Voltaire, 1767**

THE 'TRUE' NORTH STRONG AND 'FREE'

On Feb. 8, 2022, Arne and I received a nasty tasting dose of the madness that had taken over the minds of so many during the pandemic over dinner at the Bancroft Brew Pub. Soon after taking a seat in the corner by the window, a man that I recognized as one of the local conspiracy-spreading letter writers, approached our table.

"Arne!" the man said, putting his hands down heavily on the table, "Why are you wearing a mask? They don't do anything to protect you."

Looking at him in disbelief, Arne said nothing and everything without a word spoken.

"It's about protecting others," I said, doing my best to keep my mouth shut.

"Well, this whole COVID-19 thing is a hoax anyways," he said, moving in too close for comfort. "This whole thing is just Trudeau's way of turning Canada into Cuba."

"Back up," I said, pushing my chair backwards.

Thankfully, just then, seeing our annoyance with the unwanted intrusion, the waitress approached the table to take our order. Stepping back, the "freedom" fighter said goodbye to Arne, and continued on his way.

"Can I get you guys a drink to start?" the waitress asked.

"Sure, I'll have a pint of Claim Jumper."

"Me too," Arne chimed in.

"He's something else," I said. "How do you know him?"

"I don't remember," he said. "Probably the art gallery."

"We've had a few letters come in from him since the Freedom Convoy shit started going down. They were all conspiracy theory pseudoscience so they ended up in the trash can."

"Oh yeah?"

"Yeah. According to one of them our Prime Minister Justin Trudeau is really Fidel Castro's son," I said, laughing.

"Well, he was at this protest in Ottawa," said Arne. "Yesterday he phoned me in the morning, and we got into talking about this stupid stuff."

"The 'Freedom' convoy?"

"Yeah, freedom." he replied sharply. "And Karl Marx and how I like him. I told him that I'm one of those fucking Swedish socialists he hates so much. As far as these kinds of protesters go, in my books, they are all just Anarchists. I'm not too much against anarchists, because at least they usually mean well. Whereas those Nazis, they don't care at all. They just want to kill another six million Jews. He told me that if I would ask him to wear a mask he couldn't be my friend. That's how close we are."

"It's nice to have real friends," I said, shaking my head.

"I was in town for a couple of hours, and I ran into him with one of his 'freedom' fighting buddies," Arne said. "He told me that he was one of his friends from the protest. I asked if he was one of these pro-Nazi guys with the truckers. They stood together along with the Nazis in Ottawa."

"So you saw that they were flying a swastika at Parliament Hill, eh?"

"Yeah!" he barked back with contemptuous disbelief.

"Freedom of speech, right," I said. "What they really want is the freedom to hate. I suppose that gives them the 'freedom' to use what the Trumpists call 'alternative facts' too. Whatever the hell those are."

"Do you know what he said when I mentioned flying flags with swastikas on the maple leaf? He said that it was all lies. I said, 'It was on TV and reported on in all the newspapers and magazines.'

Still, he said, 'Oh, that's all lies.' Unbelievable!"

"A friend of mine sent me a picture of one of these Nazi scumbags carrying a swastika flag with a QAnon flag. I've never seen a single swastika at any of the climate justice marches or peace rallies that I've attended."

"Last night they were honking horns all night, waking people up... and that is freedom?" Arne questioned.

"For 11 days straight they've been doing it," I added. "Now there's a class action lawsuit against the truckers."

"Good. I hope so," Arne said. "You know, when you think of the way they are blocking off traffic in Ottawa and little towns; what if there is a fire and the fire truck can't get in there? They've been blocking whole cities."

"It's crazy. They're carrying gas cans, full of fuel for the truckers right outside Parliament Hill. Think of the hell you could raise with hundreds of litres of gas."

"What was the gas for?" he asked.

"They're using it to keep the trucks running so they can stay warm. So they're getting people who support them to bring it into the so-called Red Zone," I said. "If the cops spotted anyone carrying gas cans at any of the protests I've been to, they'd be shot or put in some prison or hospital to suffer for your intended "act of violence." But in Ottawa now they're letting them do whatever they want. There was a clip on the news last night that showed a bunch of people carrying gas cans walking right by the cops. And the cops just stood there smiling. It's absolutely nuts."

"I'd hate to be a cop right now," Arne said, "because there are all these laws, but they have not been tested in court."

"I wouldn't ever want to be a cop," I said. The way things are going, I can't see why anyone would want to. I think there are going to be a ton of changes to the way we live that a lot of people aren't going to be too happy with when we finally get out of this pandemic."

"I think so too," he responded. "There's so much happening and some eyes will get opened. That's what I tried to tell our friend.

I said, 'Look, in Sweden we have what you would call dirty socialism, but it works. So why would we stick with that capitalist idea when a capitalist system with a socialist government can work very well. The Swedish economy was actually 80 per cent capitalist, but they have a very strong socialist philosophy guiding them. They know what they're doing, these fucking Socialists. It's these stupid Anarchists, like this lady who get carried away. Honking horns and waking up people that are trying to sleep is no way to bring about positive change."

"There's hospitals in the area, seniors, children," I said. "I've been to a lot of protests and anytime anyone tries to set up some sort of barricade or camp, the police come in with the pepper spray and the tear gas to disperse it. I don't understand why they're giving them free reign over the national capital. It doesn't make sense. Shit! I was filming at a protest in Quebec City and I got shot with rubber bullets ... and tear gassed, several times ... just for holding a camera! At least I caught it all on tape. Hell of a lot of good it did," I added, laughing.

"We are constantly on the verge of a sort of police state situation," Arne said, "because, see, with all the media attention, etc. There's a different focus nowadays too, that is counter to Democracy."

"This is what I'm trying to understand," I said. "They say 'Freedom' convoy, but what does all this noise have to do with freedom?"

"That's what I was trying to tell this guy yesterday when we were on the phone," he said.

"An Unknown Soldier", *Arne Roosman*, watercolour on paper, 1995.

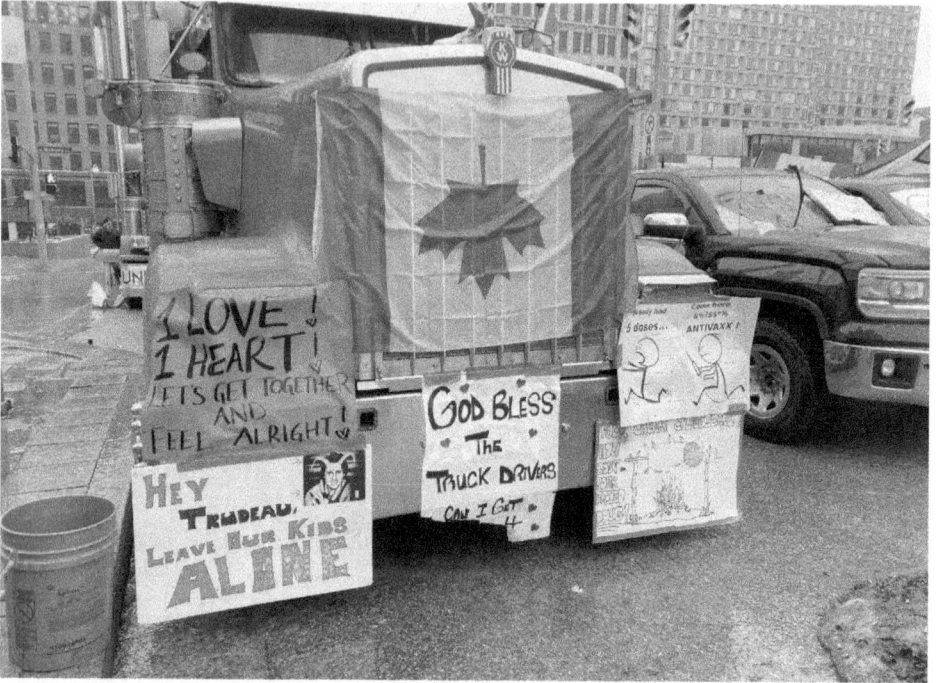

"Freedom Convoy", *N. Smelle,* photograph, February 17, 2022.

Insufficient facts always invite danger.
— Spock, 1967

TRUCKLOADS OF CONSPIRACIES

Returning home from Ottawa, I decided to take the long way home by following a network of backroads to Bancroft. Using the extra time on the road to process the parade of ignorance and hatred I had experienced, I thought of the similarities between fascist movements such as: the Vaps Movement in Estonia, Lapua Movement in Finland, the Nazis, and, of course Trump's MAGA cult in the U.S.A., eagerly standing back and standing by to do their favourite Messiah's bidding. At the core of each of these uprisings were three key elements:

1. An irrational fear of the other to facilitate an "Us versus Them" mentality.

2. The designation and demonization of an "enemy" to justify their hate, and any political violence necessary for said movement to achieve complete control over the population.

3. A fake fight for "freedom" to rally the support of the uneducated and ignorant, which on all too many occasions has proven to be enough to accomplish their goals.

There was a sort of unspoken honesty, albeit a sign of his fatal hubris, when Hitler declared, "What luck for the rulers that men do not think."[8] Likewise, in a sort of admission of guilt, Donald Trump echoed his hero's sentiment at a rally in Nevada on February 24, 2016 when he boasted, "I 'LOVE' the poorly educated!"

As always, I kept a pen and notebook beside me on the passenger seat, along with my camera in case I should be compelled to pull over and capture snapshots of anything beautiful or strange.

Regretting my decision to skip breakfast as I made my way home, I pulled over on the side of what I assumed was an unnamed abandoned logging road near Strains Lake to scarf down a couple sandwiches I had left in the cooler. Following a deer trail down to the shore, I brushed the snow off a fallen spruce tree beside the frozen lake and took a seat. Admiring the view as I sat there filling my belly, I thought about the strength of the convictions of the science deniers who were willing to believe fear-mongering politicians. These convictions were contradictory to the consensus among the overwhelming majority of the scientific community worldwide regarding the pandemic and the climate crisis, and all the world's top scientists. I thought about how much true freedom these individuals were exercising when they orchestrated the criminal and seditious invasion of our National Capital. I thought about freedom and how these individuals would define it.

Contemplating all these things and their implications for democracy, I remembered my conversation with Arne about "freedom" earlier that month, and began putting the bones together for what would eventually become my weekly column. With the fragility of freedom we discussed in mind, in the editorial I wrote:

---

8   "Hitler Quotes." 2025.
"Ivana Trump told her lawyer Michael Kennedy that from time to time her husband [Donald Trump] reads a book of Hitler's collected speeches, "My New Order," which he keeps in a cabinet by his bed."
Karl, Jonathan. 2023.

Now when I see a Canadian flag, I sadly no longer feel a sense of pride. Instead, I find myself asking: why is the self-professed "patriot" feeling compelled to let their freak flag fly? What definition of "freedom" are they proudly defending? Is it the freedom for all people on Turtle Island to have access to clean drinking water? Or is it the "freedom" that takes no issue with allowing the people of the Neskantaga First Nation to live under a boil water advisory for some 27 years? Is it the freedom for Indigenous people to set up a blockade along one of Canada's mainline train routes to protect their ancestral lands from the destruction of pipelines built for the profits of the few? Or, is it the "freedom" to disrupt the economy of the nation's capital, and cost taxpayers $11 million a day – $264-million in total – to fight for their right to party without a mask and put people's health in jeopardy?
–Nate Smelle, "The other 'F' word", in *Bancroft This Week*, 2022.

"A 'Friendly' Touch", *Arne Roosman,* mixed media on paper, 2021.

*"The Freedom Convoy is peacefully protesting
the harsh policies of far left lunatic Justin Trudeau,
who has destroyed Canada with insane Covid mandates."*
– Donald Trump, 2022

WANNABE DICTATORS, 'ALTERNATIVE FACTS' AND ELECTION INTERFERENCE

The waitress came back and took our order, after about 20 minutes. As we waited for the food to arrive, we continued our conversation regarding the far-right's persistent efforts to usurp the reins in the never-ending fight for 'Freedom.'

"Did you see that our buddy Donald McRonald is going to make a run for the White House? He has started holding campaign-style rallies again. He has been going after his former vice president Mike Pence – the same Mike Pence he was OK with his supporters hanging outside the Capitol building on January 6, last year."

"Yeah, he's been dropping hints," Arne said. "He made some comment where he was calling on his supporters to step in, if he got indicted and ended up being threatened with prison time. If there were repercussions for the insurrection on January 6th, he said there would be an even bigger insurrection. He said his supporters wouldn't accept it, and there'd be chaos in the U.S."

"So basically, he said 'If you put me behind bars there's going to be a civil war.' There's Democracy for you. Real American justice!"

"I am re-reading a book I bought about 20–30 years ago. It's a book by one very Noble German from Eastern Germany who is a landholder from an ancient family," Arne said. "He was totally anti-Nazi, because he knew Hitler personally. He was an upper-class nobleman, he knew everybody, knew everything and hated it all. He wanted nothing to do with the Nazi movement; called Hitler a dog, writing it all into his memoir, which was published in the '60s. So, with all these things going on now, it brought me back to the shelf. It's really amazing how he describes these people. At one instance, they were celebrating in München, which was a very important place for Hitler, because that's where the party sort of had its solid foothold. See, in Northern Germany there were mostly Communists and Socialists. In Bavaria and further south, the Nazis were strong. They would hold their party conventions in München at the Hofbräuhaus – the famous pub where Hitler and the Nazis first held meetings."

"I drank there when I was in Munich back in 2006," I said. "There was an Oompah band playing, lots of singing, and waitresses carrying a dozen or so giant steins full of beer without a tray. A real wild place."

Abruptly clearing his throat, then taking a healthy swig of beer, Arne raised his glass and began singing: *"Im himmel gibst kein beer, Drum Trinken wirs hier, und trinken wirs nicht hier, dan trinken die ander'n unser bier!"*

"I have never been to München (Munich) though," Arne said. "My hitchhiking experience down the Rhine River was something to remember. And I still do. I was in Heidelberg, and I went to Beethoven's place in Bonn, but unfortunately, I never made it to the Hofbräuhaus."

Recalling my experience of the historic beer hall, I described to Arne how the lively atmosphere of the Hofbräuhaus on the surface, was but a thin disguise for the very weird and sinister vibrations still lingering in the building. Looming over everyone's heads on the ceiling as the crowd emptied their glasses, was a swastika that had been covered up poorly with the blue checkerboard on the Bavarian flag. Also, knowing the history of the place, and how Hitler started brewing the shitstorm which led to the Second World War there, made it difficult to revel in the celebratory atmosphere.

"Did you get to see much of Germany outside of the camps?"

"Oh yeah. When I was 22, I hitchhiked around Germany, visiting places that I had been when I was there, the DP[9] camps."

---

9   Displaced Persons.

GIs GET HITLER'S BEER HALL

Beer mugs that once were used by the Nazis to toast Hitler, now hold coffee for doughnut-drinking purposes, as pictured above. Munich beer hall that was the site of Der Fuehrer's 1923 putsch has been taken over by the Red Cross as a canteen for enlisted men and officers.

Britain to Retain Emergency Powers

British Labor Government intends to retain wartime emergency powers possibly for five years,

from the economic problems of post-war trade and reconversion to the problems of peacetime foreign policy.

Mr. Ede reminded members that the present Emergency Pow-

"GIs get Hitler's Beer Hall". *The Bancroft Times.* August 16, 1945.

"What was that like going back at 22?"

"In those five years that I had been in Sweden, half of it was already built up again. The Krauts are amazing when it comes to smashing and rebuilding. Like Mark Zuckerberg says, 'Move fast and break things. Unless you are breaking stuff, you are not moving fast enough.' Zuckerberg is a good German name anyway: Sugar Mountain, or 'Sweet Hill.' Anyway, so Hitler, every year he had a get together at the Hofbräuhaus on the 9th of November. See, these are the dates I remember, because when I was in school in Germany those few years you had to know all these bloody Nazi dates. Another was the 20th of April, 1898 when Hitler was born. So, all this is in my head, but I don't need this shit. When you're a kid and they pop it into your brain it never goes away."

"It's amazing how our mind can retain certain information."

"At one of these parties on the 9th of November, Hitler got pissed off with Keitel, his top general, because he thought Keitel was saying something that was derogatory about the party. Well Keitel is from an old military family; they've all been generals for generations. So little Mr. Keitel there said something askew that was unsupportive of the Nazis. Do you know what Hitler did? He took a bloody copper decorative urn on the table there with whatever food or drinks, and he took it, and he smashed that right into Keitel's face. That's the kind of guy that Hitler was. He would lose his temper, but he was a regular guy off the street. He didn't make it into the academy in Vienna because he didn't take the exams. He was a fairly accurate artist. Very conventional though, and that's why he didn't get into the academy. He had nothing new to give."

"I recall seeing a few of his paintings and they were nothing special."

"There was nothing artistic about his work, but it was well-ex ecuted."

"He painted postcards and sold them on the street, didn't he?"

"Oh yeah, that's true," Arne confirmed. "The people materialized the leader who many believed would 'give us Germany back;' ... as if somebody was taking it away from the people. For Adolf it was the Jews who had taken it away from the Germans."

"A convenient enemy to blame Germany's troubles on."

"In Catholic school as a kid, every morning was the same drill: First it was the national anthem, then the Lord's Prayer. They would teach us that we're supposed to be afraid of God when we read the Bible. Then they would tell us that God is Love. This never added up for me, but they discouraged us from asking too many questions. Didn't you say it was always Hitler before Jesus with your teachers in Schwerin?"

"Well, Hitler himself was a baptized Roman Catholic. Roman Catholicism as you call it is one of the most effective tools for manipulating a larger population. The Roman Catholic Church has been tremendously successful in twisting people's minds right into their doctrine. Now, whether you like your Gods and believe is beside the point; but, just from a straight societal, human situation as we know it, it has been one of the most successful instruments. Our best invention is a 'God', you know ... and then there's the four wheels."

"A convenient ally whenever you need to justify a genocide. I remember George W. Bush saying something about God being on their side when he led the U.S.A. into Iraq. So 'God' is down with dropping bombs on innocent people?"

"I guess this 'God' doesn't mind little children getting killed," Arne said.

"As long as they're brown enough," I said.

"That's how we are," he replied. "And sadly enough, I have to concede that's how 'we' are. I'm part of the 'we' because I'm part of humanity. I can't stop it. We can reject it and not actively be in on it, but I can't avoid it because a lot of things that I do, or try to do, or even impress in my democratic fashion through voting systems, etc., a lot is still very strongly supportive of a God-like manipulative power."

"Are you guys up for another drink?" the waitress asked as she set our food down at the table.

"Yes, I am," said Arne. "Thank you."

"Me too please. Thanks."

"What really bothers me with these anarchists is how they don't understand that if they are protesting against these kind of things where there are no laws telling them not to do it, they are just creating a reason to make more laws. And more laws means less freedom. So they are advocating for more freedom, but they're creating the opposite."

With the truckers making all this noise after midnight, they sure aren't making any friends with the locals," I said.

"It doesn't make sense, Nate. They are putting all this pressure on the government, for what? The freedom to honk their horns? They will have more laws to fight next time around. They keep asking for more and more freedom and all that means is more police, enforcers, judges, court houses, etc. to accommodate their freedom to honk their horns."

"Imagine living downtown and having to deal with all this," I said. "What about all the tourists who saved up to visit the nation's capital and then had to spend their vacation sitting up all night? The whole thing reeks of Trump's MAGA bull shit."

"Oh yeah! I think it will be the demise of the so-called 'progressive' Conservative," he said.[1]

"They're hopeless. Of course enough people will still vote for them here in HLAT[2], but I don't think hitching their wagon to the convoy will help them in the long run."

"No, me neither."

"It's too bad. It seemed like Erin O'Toole and Patrick Brown were making a half assed effort to move the party more to the centre. At least with what they were saying to potential voters. Now it seems like the whole party is trying to help Trump Make America

---

[1] Derek Sloan was the former Conservative MP in HLAT from 2019-2021. Sloan ran for the leadership of the Conservative Party in 2020, however he was defeated by Erin O'Toole—a more centrist candidate like Patrick Brown. Sloan was given the boot from the Conservative Party by O'Toole on January 20, 2021 for accepting a donation from the notorious Canadian white supremacist Paul Fromm.

[2] HLAT refers to Hastings-Lennox & Addington-Tyendinaga Canadian electoral district.

Great Again."

"That's who they are now," Arne fired back.

"Did you see the cowboy on horseback with the Trump 2024: Make America Great Again flag?" I asked him.

"No, but they were talking about him on the radio. That's like that stupid guy who ran here."

"Derek Sloan?"

"Yeah! When he was running last time, he visited a friend's shop in Coe Hill, and she actually kicked him out. I had heard the story before but she told it to me recently face to face."

"What happened?"

"Well, this Sloan guy comes into her store and he was talking about how much he likes Trump; spreading his propaganda to try and get elected. She told him to get out, and that she didn't want that bull shit in her store," Arne said laughing.

"Up here, he probably figured playing the Trump card would work in his favour."

"Where is this guy now?" he asked.

"He kind of just disappeared. He tried to start his own party in the last election with his wife Jennifer but it didn't go so well."

"Big mistake!"

"I think they were banking on the far right being stronger than it actually is in Canada."

"Good riddance!" said Arne, raising his glass.

Now Mr. Poilievre already has a house in Ottawa, but by moving into Rockcliffe – one of the most exclusive neighbourhoods in the country – he gets a 19-room mansion, servants, a personal chef, and $170,000 a year in upkeep for the joint. Talk about gatekeepers, this guy's got groundskeepers.

Now personally I don't have a problem with an official residence for the leader of the opposition. But I do have a problem with Pierre Poilievre telling senior citizens that they don't deserve to have access to free public dental care, while he's being served eggs benedict from his own personal chef, in his own mansion paid for by the taxpayer.

Pierre, enough with the champagne and caviar dreams, please.

—Charlie Angus, 2023

"Arne", photograph by *N. Smelle*, September 16, 2021.

105

"A Touch of History (The Long Ago)" *Arne Roosman*, 2021.

THE MAPLE MAGA AND CON

An article on Pierre Poilievre and the federal Conservatives in the April 2022 edition of *MacLean's* magazine by Shannon Proudfoot pointed out that "Nearly every one of the affronts to freedom that Poilievre listed came from pandemic restrictions enacted by the provinces and not Prime Minister Justin Trudeau's federal Liberal government, but that was very much beside the point. 'Freedom, not fear. Truckers, not Trudeau,' he hollered over the horns that would soon torment Ottawa residence for days and sleepless nights" (Proudfoot 2022).

The article provided insight into what the Leader of Canada's Official Opposition stands on guard for, and how he earned his place at the rear end of the Conservative Party of Canada.

"Why do we need an 'Official Opposition'?" Arne questioned, as we went over some notes he made throughout the article for me. "Who are they opposing? We should be cooperating with each other, not 'officially opposing' one another."

Until that moment, I had previously considered the role of the "Official Opposition" – especially that of its Leader – as a sort of balancing agent to keep the government from moving too far in either direction on the political spectrum. Reconsidering my take in light of the insight Arne had to offer, I could now see how the very name of this role in our government is counterproductive to our national interests. As Arne suggested, if our government is meant to serve all Canadians, then essentially the role of the "Official

Opposition" is to oppose, or impede, block, fight, etc., the interests of most Canadians.

Of course I understand the benefit of having a variety of voices representing a diversity of perspectives. Today, under Poilievre's "leadership" the House of Commons has grown more combative than ever. In a similar manner to what we are seeing with MAGA Republicans in the U.S.A., any attempts at bipartisan cooperation have been squashed and replaced with name calling and a blatant disregard for science and fact when trying to "work together."

That was my main issue with the "Freedom" convoy: preventable ignorance. Every single one of the people I have met who supported the convoy's efforts in the winter of 2022 has been more willing to believe conspiracy theories that have been proven wrong over and over and over again, than they were to trust irrefutable facts produced by a scientific community consisting of the best minds in the world, and representing all countries and communities on the planet. And from what we have seen so far, our current "Leader of the Official Opposition" would rather pander to these willfully ignorant opportunists by promising to "Axe the Tax"–a carbon pricing system designed to offset the costs in healthcare and lost resources to the country by the oil companies responsible for the pollution–and "Fuck Trudeau."[10]

---

10   Editor's Note: This refers to a campaign in Canada in 2021 in which black flags bearing the words "Fuck Trudeau" were displayed on cars and houses. The phenomenon reflected a broader global trend of public frustration during the Covid-19 pandemic, when many incumbent governments faced backlash and electoral defeat across the world. Contributing factors included prolonged lockdown fatigue, sustained high inflation eroding purchasing power, stagnant wages that failed to keep pace with living expenses, widening wealth inequality, and ongoing challenges in housing affordability and job market stability.

According to Proudfoot, in university Poilievre submitted a 2,500 essay to a contest, entitled, "Building Canada through freedom." In his submission, he wrote:

> Although we Canadians seldom recognize it, the most important guardian of our living standards is freedom. The freedom to earn a living and share the fruits of our labour with loved ones, the freedom to build personal prosperity through risk-taking and strong, work ethic, the freedom of thought and speech, the freedom to make personal choices, and the collective freedom of citizens to govern their own affairs democratically.
> **–Pierre Poilievre, "Building Canada through freedom", in "Pierre Poilievre on his combative style of politics and his plans for Canada." in** *MacLean's Magazine,* **Shannon Proudfoot.**

Witnessing Poilievre cozy up with far-right extremists, conspiracy theorists, and white supremacists since announcing his support for the "Freedom" convoy in 2022 had me wondering where he stood now in terms of what he wrote in university. I wondered whether he would defend the freedom of the hard-working local business owners, workers, and residents of downtown Ottawa to, as he once wrote, "earn a living and share the fruits of [their] labour with loved ones."

What about the freedom of every Canadian—including those whose ability to earn a living was limited by the illegal occupation—to "build personal prosperity through risk-taking and strong work ethic?"

From everything Poilievre has shown us throughout his political career, especially since he decided to hitch his trailer to the herd of cosplaying "J-Sixers" responsible for the "freedom" convoy,[11]

---

11   Even before Pierre Poilievre was officially the Conservative Party's leader, he began aligning himself with far-right extremists like Jeremy Mackenzie, who suggested that members of the Canadian Freedom Convoy follow in the footsteps

there is good reason to worry about where Poilievre would personally draw the lines in terms of the limits of freedom of thought and speech.

With the Conservative Party still betting on Poilievre despite his less than underwhelming performance in the 2025 federal election, Canadians must not ignore how closely his ideology aligns with that of Trump's so called "America First" agenda. Before electing such an impostor in a blue collar to our nation's highest office, every Canadian must ask themselves: can we really trust Poilievre to protect our rights and freedoms? Will he defend a woman's right to bodily autonomy? Or will he follow the lead of his MAGA puppet masters south of the border, and push for a nationwide ban on abortion? When Poilievre heads out on the campaign trail during the next federal election in Canada, will he use his platform to denounce president Donald Trump's claim that the 2020 U.S. election was stolen —claims that have repeatedly been proven false —as an attack on the "collective freedom of citizens to govern their own affairs democratically?"

Like both Trump and Poilievre, Hitler understood the power of misinformation and how effective a weapon it was for manipulating the minds of the citizenry.[12]

"Propaganda was everywhere," explained Arne. In the newspapers, on posters around Schwerin, in movies, and on the radio, the Nazis used every media available to disseminate their disinformation campaign. Within a period of six years the number of radios in Germany grew from four million in 1933 to 16-million in 1943. Arne said it was "...the best way to reach the most people as quickly as possible."

In the June 11, 2022 edition of *The Economist* that Arne sent

---

of Trump's 'J-Sixers' and "assemble gallows on f—ing Parliament" (Gilmore 2022).

12   From Hitler's last will and testament, dictated to his secretary Traudl Junge in his Berlin Führerbunker on April 29, 1945: "It is not truth that matters, but victory.", Hitler Quotes 2025.

me home with after our previous meeting, an article entitled "The Insurrection Televised" pointed out how Trump's campaign to overthrow the election was publicized in great detail at the time. Evidence of his seditious conspiracy was turned over to the media in an audio recording where the former president can be heard pressuring Georgia's Secretary of State to "find 11,780 votes." The article described that now infamous day in American history:

> The riot that ensued was broadcast live and was so obviously the culmination of Mr. Trump's efforts that even most Republican leaders at first said as much. Kevin McCarthy, the Republican leader of the house, at the time, said publicly that the former president was responsible, and told colleagues, he would instruct Mr. Trump to resign. Yet it quickly transpired that most Republican voters preferred Mr. Trump's version of reality to the evidence of their eyes. So Mr. McCarthy, and most other Republican lawmakers backpedaled, leaving Ms. Cheney and Mr. Kinzinger, among the few in their party willing to stand against insurrection.
> **- "The Insurrection Televised", in *The Economist*, 2022.**

In the wake of the attack on the Capitol, several slick Republicans smelled blood in the water—Trump's blood—and at the time some even had the courage to take a nibble. January 7, the day after the insurrection, Republican Senator for South Carolina, Lindsey Graham, told his fellow lawmakers, "When it comes to accountability, the President needs to understand that his actions were the problem, not the solution, that the rally yesterday was unseemly, it got out of hand... I said on the floor of the Senate, I cast my vote accordingly, that Joe Biden is the legitimate president-elect of the United States." A little more than a month later on February 13, Senate Minority Leader and Senator from Kentucky "Moscow" Mitch McConnell stated, "January 6th was a disgrace... American citizens attacked their own government. They used terrorism to try to stop a specific piece of democratic business they did not like... Fellow Americans beat and bloodied our own police. They stormed the Senate floor. They tried to hunt down the Speaker of the House. They built gallows and chanted about murdering the Vice President... They did this because they had been fed wild falsehoods by the most powerful man on Earth — because he was angry, he'd lost an election."

By June 1, 2024, in spite of Trump's conviction on 34 counts of falsifying business records to pay off porn star Stormy Daniels, to hide the affair they had four months after his wife Melania gave birth to their son Baron, Republicans —including Graham, McCarthy, McConnell, as well as a long list of others Trump has humiliated in public such as Ron DeSantis, Ted Cruz, Nikki Haley—have all knelt

"Touch me not (Banned on Blue Sky/It's not porn)", *Arne Roosman,* mixed media on paper, 2021.

down in front of their Master and kissed the ring.

Shame does not exist in the Republican Party of today, nor integrity, honesty, or basic common sense. All that remains is an insatiable lust for power; and depressingly that just might be enough to give them the keys to the kingdom, along with all the authority they need to change the locks and do away with democracy in the free world. Sadly, for us here north of the border, as is sometimes the case with elections in Canada, our copycat Conservative Party is content with following in the Americans' footsteps.

"Shhh... Not in my face/The Art of the Kneel", *Arne Roosman,* mixed media on paper, 2021.

Hitler observed that most demagogues are timid,
and so venture only small lies which are found out because the masses,
also petty-minded, can see through the retail lying they do themselves;
but the masses will accept the 'big lie' because they cannot imagine anyone daring
enough to try it.
– Dwight Macdonald, 1962

WHERE THERE'S SMOKE, THERE'S FIRE

With the smell of wildfire smoke still lingering in the air, Arne and I met for dinner in Bancroft on September 13, 2023, to catch up and talk about the increasing presence of Nazis in global politics. As he expressed his frustration with the fact that Nazis were still even a part of the conversation in 2023, we sat there on the patio of The Granite, enjoying the warmth of the sun and how it blended perfectly with the cool autumn breeze.

"I love that painting of yours," I said, pointing to his mural on the York River side of the building on Bridge Street.

"Thank you. It is starting to fade though. It really should be touched up," he said.

"It looks good to me, but you know what it should look like."

"Yeah, the orange especially needs touching up."

"Just like in the U.S. I can think of something orange down there in need of some serious touch ups."

"Ho! Ho!" he laughed. "But I think he needs more than a touch up. He's going to bring down the whole bloody country with his fucking lies."

"It's scary to see how fast the States are going backwards," I said, taking in the last big gulp of warm beer in my glass.

"And at full speed." said Arne.

"Hey! On the bright side, it's looking more and more like our buddy Donald might actually have to face some consequences for all his bullshit."

"I hope so," he said. "I hope they lock him up. They should

lock him up for a few years."

"At least until after the election. He's done more than enough to earn a couple years behind bars."

"Just give him two years in jail and that's all we need to get him off this political bullshit."

"He's not coming back after that," I added.

"No. That's all we need. I just read in this weekend's New York Times that there's a couple of simple cases that would put him away, that has put people away for two years. And that's really all we need: two years of no Trump. Those who are still crying about him, they can keep on crying forever because those two years would make him a president who was in prison. A criminal!"

"Yeah, this is his last chance to destroy the country completely," I said.

"Freedom may never be conceived merely negatively, as the absence of compulsion. Freedom conceived intersubjectively distinguishes itself from the arbitrary freedom of the isolated individual. No one is free until we are all free."
- Jürgen Habermas, 2014

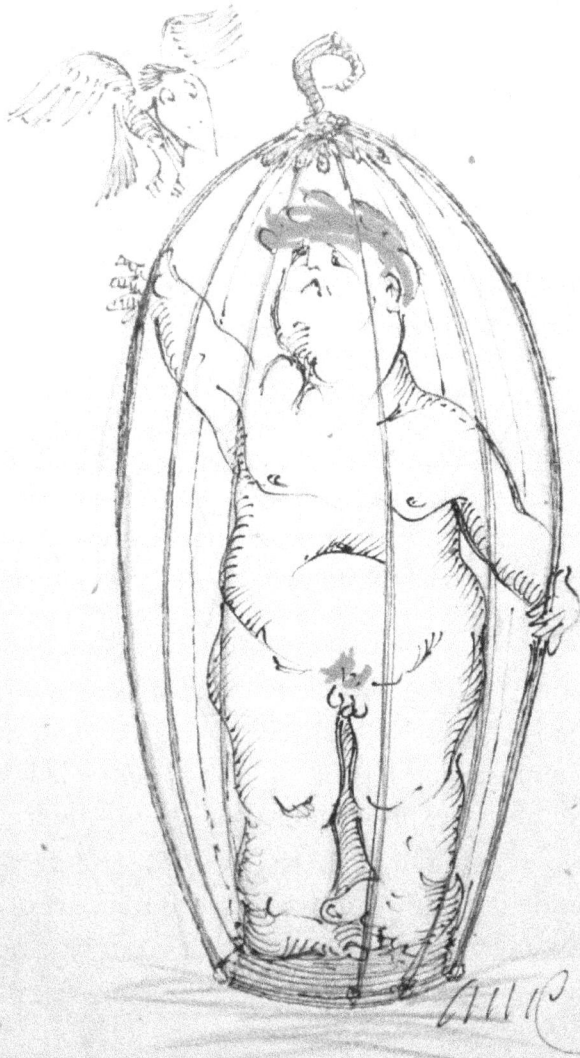

THIS BIRDMAN [SING SING] NO SONG, AND ALCATRAZ IS OCCUPIED.

"A Taste of Freedom", *Arne Roosman,* mixed media on paper, 2021.

"I don't know Nate; this Trump guy is a caricature of a lot of political happenings. It's really unbelievable that this kind of guy can achieve this kind of prominence and become part of history. That is very much what pushes him on. He wants to be a biblical figure. Well, he will last for 1,000 years now."

"Isn't that a nasty fucking thought. It's true, though, even when this bozo is long gone, his legacy of hate and greed worship will continue."

Arne expressed his frustration with Trump and those who choose to overlook his history of degrading and sexually assaulting women and still vote for him. I showed him a video on my cell phone of a neo-Nazi gang in Florida that had taken over a bridge near Disney World. Waving flags bearing swastikas, along with others demanding to," Make America Great Again" — a common and apparently comfortable combination of movements in both Canada and the U.S.A. — the mostly skinhead mob unleashed their cowardly fury on the passing traffic.

"Heil Hitler!" the trashy pale lynch mob screamed. "Sieg heil! Sieg heil! Sieg heil!"; "Jews will not replace us! Jews will not replace us!"; "Faggot, faggot, faggot, faggot, ...," the Nazis yelled in rage as a man crossing the bridge expressed his disgust with their existence.

"What's happening here?" Arne asked worriedly. "They look like Nazis," he added, without yet having seen the part of the video where the swastika was visible.

"Yeah, unreal eh! Loud and proud Nazis in 2024. Really something to be proud of."

"This is America today," he said looking down into his beer glass with disappointment. Noticing his eyes beginning to fill with water, I felt bad for showing him the video.

"What gets me is that they have Trump and DeSantis flags."

"This DeSantis ... if ever there was a fake."

"How is it possible that we as a society after another 80 years — eight decades that have arguably seen the most social progress in the history of humanity — are still so consumed by hate?" I asked Arne.

Shaking his head in disgust, he said, "They feel justified in doing it. They don't think they are doing a horrible thing. No, no! They are just showing that with their political colouring it is proper to hang someone from a post if you don't agree with their politics. Just like these guys on the bridge, there is nothing wrong with Trump or DeSantis. At the same time, these are the same bums, always crying about your freedom being taken away by liberal snowflakes. Fuck, they live in a country that is free enough to have a public Nazi circle jerk. How much more freedom do they need?"

We sat there for an hour or more so, talking about the 2024 U.S.A. election, wondering whether Trump would even be allowed to run after his botched revolution on January 6, 2021. Laughing at the ridiculousness of America's political landscape since 2016— more specifically about the latest episode in the MAGA soap opera in which a handful of Trumplicans were attempting to impeach President Joe Biden, because from what I can tell, his son Hunter enjoyed hookers and blow too much.

"This is how naive they are," he said.

"This kind of naivety works with voters on the far right, right wing, whatever wings you have. If there is an impeachment, then he— Joe Biden, or whoever is in the president's chair—is a bad guy."

"And this is America, the greatest democracy of all time."

"Then we have our other good buddy Poilievre[13]..."

"There's another one!" he said. "Do you know what is funny about this guy? He is such a caricature. They told him that he looks stupid in glasses, so what does he do? Well, all of a sudden he does not wear his glasses anymore."

"We're in high school again."

"It's such a stupid reaction. Who says people who wear glasses don't look smart? At least 50 per cent of our population wears glasses; anybody over 65."

---

13   The Maple MAGA Leader of the Conservative Party of Canada during the tenure of Liberal Party of Canada Prime Minister Justin Trudeau.

"If there's a God in Ottawa Jagmeet Singh will give him a wedgie and steal his lunch money."

"I just can't imagine him becoming a prime minister," Arne said. "Then 'Oh Canada' becomes 'No Canada.'"

"Happy Canada Day!" (Filly and Trooper series), *Arne Roosman,* oil on wood panel, 2022.

"Vive le Canada!" (Filly and Trooper series), *Arne Roosman*, pencil on paper, 2022.

GŒBBELS: "YOU MUST BELIEVE WHAT THE FÜHRER SAYS, NOT YOUR EYES..."

Cartoon from the Cartoon Comment.

"Misinformation", cartoon in *The Bancroft Times,* January 8, 1942.

Today around the world, demagogues appeal to our worst instincts.
Conspiracy theories once confined to the fringe are going mainstream.
It's as if the Age of Reason—the era of evidential argument—is ending,
and now knowledge is delegitimized, and scientific consensus is dismissed.
Democracy, which depends on shared truths, is in retreat,
and autocracy, which depends on shared lies, is on the march.
Hate crimes are surging,
as are murderous attacks on religious and ethnic minorities.
– Sacha Baron Cohen, 2019

NO CANADA: OUR HOME ON NATIVE LAND

On Aug. 26, 2023, about a week before the cosplaying American Nazis had taken over the bridge in Orlando, Florida, three people were murdered– shot to death in a Dollar General store in Jacksonville, Florida– by a masked man with a swastika painted on his gun. These types of violent hate crimes and speech have been on the rise ever since Trump was first elected in 2016.

An FBI report published in *Newsweek* shortly after Americans ended Trump's dream of remaining in the White House in 2020, revealed that "hate-motivated murders, largely committed by white supremacists, spiked to their highest number in 28 years" (Villarreal 2020). During the 2020 U.S. election Trump really leaned into his support from the far-right and conspiracy theorists. Throughout the campaign he steadily ramped up his use of violent, racist, anti-immigrant and anti-Democratic rhetoric to mobilize his base.

Despite the complete lack of evidence proving that the 2020 election was, as Trump falsely claimed, "stolen", his blatant lies inspired the "Stop the Steal" campaign. In turn, these lies gave rise to the MAGA mob's attempt to overthrow the government of the United States of America on January 6, 2021. Spreading over the border like a pandemic, roughly a year later, a relatively small but loud faction of copycats in Canada – often referred to as "Maple-MAGA" – who harboured a similar kind of hatred for immigrants, diversity and inclusion, publicly funded health care and education, and clean air and water as their southern neighbours, staged

123

their own attack on the government of Canada, with the illegal occupation of downtown Ottawa by the "Freedom" convoy.

Echoing the sentiment of those who stormed the U.S. Capitol buildings in Trump's name a year earlier, Pat King, one of the organizers of the convoy, posted a video online ahead of the convoy's arrival in Ottawa promoting a favourite conspiracy of white supremacists known as the "Great Replacement Theory." Knowingly vomiting misinformation, King presented the racist myth of an ongoing "white genocide" to his followers, stating, "…what there is, is there's an endgame, called 'de-population of the Caucasian race … or the Anglo-Saxons. And that's what the goal is, is to de-populate the Anglo-Saxon race, because they are the ones with the 'strongest' bloodline" (YouTube 2022).

This is the same race replacement conspiracy theory that was cited as the motive by the 18-year-old white supremacist mass shooter, Payton Gendron, before he entered a Topps Supermarket in Buffalo, New York and murdered 10 innocent Black people because of the colour of their skin.[14]

Just as they were during the insurrection in Washington, D.C. in January 2021, these deadly ideologies, powered by hate, were at the very core of the forces behind the convoy. Jason LaFace, one of the main organizers of the three-week long occupation, is also known to be associated with the far-right, anti-immigrant group from Finland, the Soldiers of Odin. Founder of the Canadian far-right extremist group Diagolon, Jeremy Mackenzie is yet another racist convoy clown with nefarious intentions regarding Democracy in Canada.

The Conservative's leader Poilievre has been seen getting cozy with MacKenzie on camera, even marching alongside one of his podcast guests, James Topp, another well-known Canadian far-right extremist.

---

14   Included in Edited Final Bibliography: "Buffalo shooting suspect says his motive was to prevent 'eliminating the white race'". The Associate Press. June 16, 2022. https://www.npr.org/2022/06/16/1105776617/buffalo-shooting-suspect-says-his-motive-was-to-prevent-eliminating-the-white-ra

In September of 2022 it appeared as if there may have been a falling out between Poilievre and his new far-right buddies, due to a video taken by some of the Conservative leader's fans at an "Axe the Tax" protest in Nova Scotia. During MacKenzie's podcast, he said to his guest on the show, Alex Vriend, speaking of Poilievre's wife, "let's rape her! It's not really a sex thing. It's like we just want to show people that we can do things to you if we want to. It's a power move" (Raycraft 2022). For some men, such vile threats made toward the person he loves in public and online would be enough reason to abandon his relationship with far-right extremists, or at the very least with Diagolon; this was not the case with Poilievre. In spite of MacKenzie's threats made less than two years earlier, Poilievre can be seen meeting with supporters of the group in an RV that had a drawing of the black and white Diagolon flag on the door. During the meeting *CBC* reported that Poilievre can be seen in a video that shows protesters with "Axe the tax" and "F--k Trudeau" signs and flags, as well as a car with the words "Make Canada Great Again" scrawled on the rear window, telling his far-right supporters, "People believed his lies. Everything he [Former Prime Minister Justin Trudeau] said was bullshit, from top to bottom" (Tunney 2024).

The federal government has confirmed that hate crimes have been on the rise in Canada in a report on its website. The report acknowledges that hate crimes in Canada had "increased 72 per cent between 2020 and 2021 due to increases in hate crimes targeting religion, sexual orientation, and race or ethnicity" (Ndegwa/ McDonald 2023). The study also recognized that all provinces and territories in Canada, except for Yukon, reported increased numbers of hate crimes in 2021. Attesting to Trump's role in provoking this rapidly accumulating threat of violent hate crimes, the study shows how after the orange anti-Christ[15] took office in 2016, the number of such incidents had more than doubled by 2021, climbing from 1,409 in 2016 to 3,360.

---

15   Some Christians believe Trump is the anti-Christ, and they desire for him to bring about the apocalypse in their Book of Revelations (Maza 2018).

Helle[16] kept the original over all those years.

For the viewer, like yourself, think of yourself as an Egyptologist, facing hieroglyphics from 3,000 years ago.

Same applies to the bugs and the creature in the cart.

Trees, being fed, water pumped, with no pumper in sight — perhaps they were off filling a tree.

The trio at the bottom, seemingly military commander, commanded by an officer at the bottom right.

Viewer, make up your story.

You won't be far off whatever your conclusion, in the pre-TV days.

We grew up with bugs.

Bedbugs, pre-DDT, people collected bugs in big flat display boxes, needled down.

Arsenic was applied, to prevent them from being eaten by other cannibal minded insects.

–Arne Roosman

Arne Roosman's mother.

Lapsepõlv, Arne Roosman, crayon on paper, 1939.

127

13 YEARS OF DARKNESS

At four-years-old, the politics of war controlling Arne and his family's existence, unbeknownst to him, he said, was nothing but a collection of names floating around his "anarchist's brainscape." Extracting words from his memories of early childhood, he recalls:

Stalin's Molotov cocktail, Hitler the vegetarian, both marching in uniforms. Hitler Youth, Nurses, Airbeitsdienst the Unions, also in uniforms; more of the same. The Luftwaffe, Wehrmacht, Keiegesmarine, the SS, the Brownshirts; more and more music carrying Wagnerian harmonies all the way.
–Arne Roosman, 2022

Arriving in a world becoming more and more shrouded in darkness with every passing day, Arne's light started shining on the sunny morning of Sunday, March 6, 1932. Born into the Kurjamäe Clan of the ancient Estonian Muddy Hill, Arne's mother Helle's side of the family was of the lineage identifying with the colonial German moniker Boesberg, sometimes spelled Bisberg. On his Papa Axel's side, only the German colonial moniker exists, Roosman: "Man of the Horse." The Estonian equivalent would be Kutsar, or "coachman." The spelling of the Roosman family name would vary depending on the political situation; transforming into Roosma, Rosmaa, Rossman, or Roosman whenever threats of being labelled as "the other side" would arise.

In early April of 2023, Arne reminisced with me about his first years in Tallinn, Estonia and what it was like for him as a child growing up amidst the poverty of war and a constant threat of political violence.

"Did someone order a pizza?" I said loudly as I knocked on Arne's partially open front door.

"Hello! Look at this," he said, opening the box I had placed in front of him on the kitchen table. "Smells good. Where is it from?"

"The Gas Station Pizzeria," I said laughing. "Hey, they make a damn good pizza. Can I get you anything else before we dig in?"

"I'll have one of those beers," Arne said, pointing to the six pack of beer I still had tucked under my arm.

"Do you need a cup?" I asked.

"No, I have everything here. Thanks."

In preparation for what we both expected to be a difficult discussion about some of the darker moments from his past, I had looked for the strongest beer in the LCBO in Coe Hill.

"This is the good stuff here, Arne. It will put some hair on your chest. It's from a brewery in Toronto."

"Boneshaker, eh! The real thing," Arne said, raising his glass. "Here's to life."

"Cheers."

Reviewing the questions that I had left him at the end of our last visit, or 'homework' as he called it, got Arne thinking about his brief time in Tallinn as a child. Reflecting on his sources of entertainment then and now, he said, "We are not in touch with the past, are we? We are the TV generation et cetera, et cetera. Now before TV, what did people do? They had nothing to do. So, what did they do? They collected bugs. My dad had a collection of bugs. Huge boxes! I remember them in big flat boxes like this. You take the bugs and you kill them with arsenic – see this is the "Touch of Arsenic" – then, with needles, you put them onto this cardboard inside the flat box. So, you put a touch of arsenic in there to keep other bugs from getting in and eating the bugs. Bugs and arsenic, they are tied together. That's why this six-year-old boy drew bugs."

"Interesting! My grandmother used to collect insects when she was a little girl in England. Would you paint or draw from his collection?"

"Yeah, but they were all over the place outside," Arne said. "Bugs were part of the regular conversation and inspiration."

"Ah! That explains all the ants and other insects crawling between the lines of your series of libelli."

"That's why then we have this huge piece of artwork," exclaimed Arne as he held up a photocopy of a drawing he had done when he was six-years old. "It's really hard to see what these guys are doing, but it's obvious for some reason. The guy who's pumping the water away from the water he's in, he's chopping down the tree, but there are two water pumps that are not attended to. And then we have this tree, you hear? They look like soldiers. You know, up here. I think they are army boys. And this guy looks like a chief of the sea. He seems to be in charge of these three. What it is really all about is a story that is lost. It's a lost story. It's kind of like Egyptian hieroglyphs. You have pictures of a story, and you need to figure out what the hell I was trying to say. I signed it for posterity."

"There's so much going on here. Where were you when you did this?"

"Well, we didn't go to school at six-years-old," Arne said. "We didn't go to school until we were seven or eight in Estonia. We lived in Keila, outside of Tallinn. We always lived outside Tallinn because all of Dad's accounts were in the capital. Mother was in hospital with my sister Marit being born," Arne said.

"She was at Grandpa's place, because he did the babysitting. He didn't have a printing shop anymore. We kept on moving for many reasons, and we had just moved into another apartment. When Marit was born that was the 24th of February, which is a very

130

important date because that is when the Republic of Estonia was proclaimed, the 24th of February 1918. So, on the 20-year anniversary of 1918 my sister was born. When the Republic was celebrating its 20-year anniversary away from the Russian and German slavery. Grandpa is babysitting and we have just moved to another address, so things were a little bit up and down. The baby was not born in the house. In the good old days in Estonia babies were born at home. She was the second one of us born in a hospital. I was the first one born in a hospital in Tallinn. So, Grandpa is babysitting the three boys, and I don't know what my older sister Ingrid was doing, but us three boys are celebrating the 20-year anniversary of our super republic. Now we are free people, we are a Republic, so Grandpa made us wooden swords, sabers; and we were marching in the living room singing important songs like the famous Finnish Anthem that is also the Estonian anthem. We made it into a marching song because really, it's a choral kind of melody."

"So it's the Finnish national anthem and the Estonian?" I asked.

"Yeah, the composer was a German and a Finn," he said. "It's a beautiful song, probably one of the most beautiful anthems there is. The melody is just perfect. See a lot of these national anthems are rather folksy or military, but this one is very musically legit."

"Tallinn", *Arne Roosman,* ink on paper, 1995.

TALLINN'S THREE LITTLE PATRIOTS

As the Russians rolled into Tallinn in June of 1940, Arne said he and his brothers — Gösta, the oldest of the Roosman trio, and Benny, the youngest — waited by the roadside to watch the line of T34 tanks as they approached the city. As the line of tanks passed by, he said the soldiers tossed a "profusion of earned and undeserved medals, and red star insignia torn off their shirts" as gifts to those who had gathered to "welcome" their arrival.

The Soviet occupation of Estonia brought with it administrators of the new proletarian breed, explained Arne. To the delight of many men and teenage boys, he said the Russians' wives would wear lingerie in public that they purchased in Tallinn, thinking it was fashionable local outerwear.

Soon after the new overlords had settled in, Arne said he and his brothers decided to launch their own resistance against the occupying Soviets. Recalling his memory of their offensive that day, he said they were "Bad little boys, doing bad things for a 'just' cause." Sensing the anxiety of their parents, Arne and his brothers magically morphed into Tallinn's Three Little Patriots when they acted on their plan to weaken the occupying forces.

Spying a cache of oil drums stashed at the forest's edge atop of a steep hill, and a row of unguarded Russian T34 tanks parked at the bottom of said hill, he said they prepared themselves to unleash a barrel full of sabotage.

According to Arne, this lack of awareness among the troops gave the Roosman trio a window of opportunity to sabotage the machinery of the Russians. While the Soviet conscripts were drinking vodka, smoking cigarettes, and dancing, he said the boys stealthily maneuvered behind their backs and crept through the forest until they reached the barrels. Prying loose the lids on each of the drums, they used all their might to tip them over and roll them downhill toward the tanks.

When asked to describe the scene of the crime that day, Arne said:

> *There was this group of happy red conscripts, sipping their seemingly inexhaustible supply of vodka. They did not give much of a damn what took place around them. The T34 Tanks were parked by the dozens behind the cloister. Oddly, the oil which kept the army moving, when necessary was stored in sizeable drums up on the hill. With considerable effort, we managed to open the lock ups, and down the hill, we rolled the juice from Baku. Squirting up in the air, down in the grass, messing up the hillside, and smashing into the war machines with a bang!*
> *K   A   B   O   O   M   !   !   !*
> **– Arne Roosman, 2022**

The political turbulence of post-First World War and pre-Second World War, melting like a snowball in one's fist, kept dripping with freshly fallen snowflakes. As Arne lay there in Helle's arms, breathing in his earliest breaths, the hot air was being sucked out of the lungs of the far-right Lapua Movement in Estonia's neighbour Finland. Arne and I had an opportunity to talk about the world he was born into and how it stacks up to today's reality, over breakfast at his place in Coe Hill on September 29, 2022.

Knock! Knock!
"Arne! How are you doing this morning? Latte, my friend!"
"Hello! Great. Just eating breakfast. Come on in."
"I brought us some coffee and sweet bread."
"Excellent. Thanks Nate."

"Little Patriots", *Arne Roosman,* conte and charcoal on paper, 2014.

"No problem. I was up late last night digging into the world you were born into, so every bit of fuel helps," I said, taking a big sip of coffee.

"So, what did you find out about 'my' world?"

"Well, it was a very interesting night," I said. "It turns out there was a far-right nationalist gang running around Finland at the time, calling themselves the Lapua Movement. Looking into what they were all about, they seemed a hell of a lot like the Proud Boys and the rest of Trump's band of deranged bullies. They reminded me of our 'Freedom' fighters here in Canada as well," I said.

"Oh yeah?"

"It's unbelievable that this shit is still going on," I said. "You would think that we would get bored with playing the same broken record. How many more times will we experiment with fascism before we realize it is a waste of our time and energy. Anyways, so these Finns had ties with the Nazis. It was a real wake up call regarding what we are up against."

Hitler took power on January 30, 1933. That was when "all kinds of things started changing," explained Arne. "People anticipated it. With anyone engaged in serious contemplation there was a lot of prophecy in the '20s and '30s by writers who saw what was happening, what was coming."

"I don't get it Arne, why the hell are we getting ourselves back into this same sort of shitstorm again when we know how it ends?"

"It's a mystery, my friend."

"When I looked at this Lapua Movement, it also reminded me of our conversation about the former Conservative Member of Parliament Maxine Bernier's People's Party of Canada. I guess this Lapua Movement started in the Village of Lapua when local Communist youth held a small parade. A bunch of these pro-fascist nutjobs basically crashed the kids parade and beat the shit out of everybody. Free speech, right?!"

When I researched what happened to the Finns' fascist 'Freedom' fighters, I learned that they were dealt with rather quickly. A couple years later in February of 1932 there was a Social Democrat meeting in Mäntsälä where a bunch of goons from the Lapua

136

Movement came in armed and staged a coup that ended up being called the Mäntsälä Rebellion. They failed of course, as fascist scum inevitably do. Once the rebellion had been squashed, every last one of the coup's leaders were arrested on March 6.

"You'll like this, Arne. After the Lapua Movement was wiped out, some of its members who were not arrested during the failed rebellion, formed the Patriotic People's Movement."

"Hmmm ... sounds familiar," Arne said.

"Jesus Christ! It's happening again, with the direction Conservatives in Canada have been heading since Trump took office in 2016, especially since his fumbled coup on January 6. And now we have our own un-Patriotic People's Party of Canada promoting the same kind of fascist agenda."

"It's nothing new, Nate. We had this party with a Finnish connection called the Vaps movement. One of my neighbour's husband's father was part of the movement. He was a cop in Tallinn. The movement was started by guys who called themselves "freedom fighters" (vaps is short for vabadussõjalased, which translates as "freedom fighter"). In 1918 they started the Republic, but then they went 'Trumpian-like' to the far-right. We had democratic elections, and our first president in Estonia was named Konstantin Päts. He didn't like what was going on with the Vaps. They were sort of stupid 'bad boys', bullies. Having been elected democratically, Päts got on the stamps and everything. He was a sort of happy, sort of stern, round-faced guy. He was part of the Russian Revolution of 1905. Being on the border, whatever affected Russia impacted Estonia, Latvia, etc.[17] When the Vaps started doing too much Trumpian kind of bullshit in Parliament, he said, 'I've had enough!' Päts took over and basically became a kind of dictator. He told all these bloody people, the Vaps, to get lost. He told them, 'If you want to come into Parliament and help us with good things like how we can feed the people, so they don't go hungry, that's fine, but don't give me that bullshit with this far right crap.' So right up until he was arrested by the Communists in 1940 and sent to Siberia, he was pretty much

---

17   Editor's Note: Päts was something of a centre-right, Doug Ford type.

running the country the way he thought was best."

"Would you say he was good for the country?"

"He was sort of like Salazar in Portugal. If someone told him something he would consider it but wouldn't take it to Parliament to discuss it forever. He'd say, 'We need action here! The people need meat, the people need bread, so let them eat.' That's the kind of leader he was. Estonians sort of accepted his dictatorship. There was actually very little movement against him."[18]

> **Editor's Note:** *The Vaps Movement wanted to replace the slow and steady Parliamentary Democracy system with an all-powerful President: "[T]he president could initiate legislation, issue decrees when the Riigikogu was not in session or in the case of 'immediate state necessity', lead cabinet meetings, and form and dismiss governments" (Kasekamp 2015). Päts was a centre-right politician who used the support of the ultra-right Vaps Movement to initiate these sweeping presidential powers, letting their armed rebellions intimidate and disrupt Parliament, and then threw them all in prison once he had secured power.*

"The Vaps were put in prison for their insurrection, sort of like Trump's supporters after the failed insurrection on January 6, 2021. Trump should be jailed, because a lot of people have been jailed on lesser charges for doing his bidding."

"He was just indicted, eh!"

"Yes, Nate. Yes! Finally!"

"Do you know what the worst thing about Trump is for me, Arne? It is that 50, 100 years down the road he's still going to be remembered as a former American president. He was elected democratically in 2016, so he'll still be a part of that club. There have

---

18   Editor's Note: many former Soviet countries were more vulnerable to dictatorship due to generations of social conditioning, even after liberation. It takes several generations of democratic tradition for post-authoritarian citizens to feel free to criticize the government, and to develop critical thinking about leaders, their promises, their slogans, and potentially their propaganda.

been some not-so-great presidents in the past, but he is going to leave a nasty stain."

"It's so sad. That's what really screws democracy, Nate. It's totally meaningless now; the idea of a democracy of the people is totally kaput. It's gone."

"I agree, the concept has lost its credibility. In a Democracy you should at least have a fair shot – one vote – to elect the leader you want. And you might not get the one you want every election, but at least there's a chance. Now, whenever a far-right candidate loses they scream 'It was rigged! Stop the Steal! It's getting ridiculous. This morning, I was watching the news, and they were talking about the Miss Universe Pageant and apparently it was rigged. Jesus, we can't get our shit together to elect Miss Universe?"

"There's no end to this, Nate."

"Next time the Leafs get the boot from the playoffs we should start a campaign saying they won the Stanley Cup. Seriously though, it's like facts don't mean anything anymore. That's the scariest part, Arne. What do you think this means for the future of democracy?"

"It's dead!" proclaimed Arne. "There was a recent headline in *Time Magazine* about Democracy and how bloody dead it is. And if you read between the lines, really it is. It's not there anymore. We must bring it back; salvage it somehow. It'll never be the same; and of course, you can argue whether it was ever there. Did we ever really have democracy? If you go by the American Constitution we probably didn't. But what we lost is a system that was reasonably functioning. We gave it a nice name, democracy, which we borrowed from ancient times, humans that gave serious thought. But they didn't let women vote either, so even our Greek and Roman connections can be faulty."

"I believe the intent was good, but there are obviously a lot of quirks that still need to be worked out," I said.

"But Nate, they always at least tried to make it better. From my understanding of reading and appreciating history, there has always been a trend among functionaries – people responsible for difficult global decisions, national decisions, etc. that they at least tried. Even if they failed, and intentionally misused the loopholes, etc. – which is also called human nature – the official line was always 'let's keep on trying.' We all know that we are not perfect. It's like if you have too much salt in your porridge; well, don't try to take the salt out and spoil the porridge, just add a little more porridge without salt, and before you know it, it is palatable. That has to be, in my books, the thinking. You can't clean out the mess, but you can add good stuff to the mess, so that the bad stuff is not that dominant. Like the porridge and the salt."

"That's an excellent analogy Arne! No use throwing out the porridge when it still holds the potential to nourish us."

"Right, the salt is still in there, but it's not that offensive anymore. The bad stuff will always be there, it will never go away. But you add a lot of good stuff and the power of the bad gets diminished by the good."

"So would it be fair to say Arne that you see democracy itself as a work in progress?"

"Yes, exactly. Right now, we have a long bad pause where we stopped that work in progress. We just sat on it as it was, and the bad boys are taking advantage of the fact that the people aren't paying close enough attention."

With the Second World War really heating up in 1939, Arne said tensions flared up in the Roosmans' homeland when Russian forces occupied Estonia. This escalation brought with it a potentially life or death decision for the Roosman family: 1) emigrate to Joseph Stalin's Russia where they could be sent to Siberia because of his paternal grandmother's German heritage; or, 2) move the family to Adolf Hitler's Germany where they would not be so harshly persecuted for his grandmother's ancient Colonial Germanic roots, but Jews were not popular.

The need for the Roosmans to decide regarding where the family would be safest became more urgent in 1940, Arne said, when "strange rumours" began surfacing about the disappearance of Jewish people in Germany. Likewise, he acknowledged that there were also disturbing reports of similar atrocities being committed in Russia.

Arne said that at the age of eight he learned that the "walls had ears." He remembers the fear he experienced when his parents taught him and his siblings to be careful with everything they said, at all times.

"There was so much political talk when we left Estonia," Arne said.

"The grown-ups were always whispering. There was always fear because when you are living in such a secret society that is sort of led by secrets and whisperings, there is a constant threat."

Roosman said every time he and his siblings heard their parents and the other adults whisper, they knew what they were talking about was important, so they would listen more keenly. Because the whispers were usually in Russian, the secret language of the adults, Arne said it was difficult to understand what was being discussed. From the tone and the timing of the whispers, however, he said he and the other children knew that whatever it was they were discussing was extremely serious.

"There are so many 'whys' and they all induce some sort of fear," Arne explained.

"Partly, I think it is a fear of the unknown, because suddenly that becomes an everyday thing for you – the anxiety."

An uncle of Roosman's had tried to immigrate to Germany in 1939 but was turned away because only his grandmother was of German descent. Arne said Hitler decided to get rid of this red tape a year later after repeated failures on the battlefield. Now considered 'German enough' under Hitler's new rules, his family decided to leave Tallinn, crossing the Baltic Sea in search of safety in his grandmother's homeland of Deutschland, now a threatening colonial power, like the Russian power bordering the eastern part of Axel Roosman's little *lapsepõlvekodu*.

Despite rising tensions in Tallinn as the war raged on, and rumours of Estonians being sent to Stalin's Siberia, Arne said Papa Axel's casual optimism towards life provided a sense of security for the family.

"We were able to brush aside the curtain of clouds, and for a while, bask in the sunshine of our illusions; some of which were really warm and real," explained Arne.

The comfort of these illusions quickly evaporated during

the Roosmans' last visit with their relatives in Tallinn before they chose to take their chances in Germany. Arne described the uneasy atmosphere at the gathering that evening:

"Dark moments, dark rooms, worried whispers. We youngsters were told we would not understand."[19]

The world was changing too fast and too furiously for even the most astute adult to make sense of. Arne and the other children were consumed by questions.

"Why was it that Uncle Hartius, in our books the greatest stage and movie actor, was deported to Siberia? Why was it that his wife, the actress Aunt Mizzi, whose Sunday broadcast for children allowed us to skip the otherwise mandatory afternoon nap, was to follow him? And why was it that their son, the dashing merchant Marine officer, was to meet the same fate?"

The family spoke Estonian and German, "but the dark whispers were in Russian," explained Arne. "Yes, one day we would understand, and it would not be the spoken word, but the language of the strange darkness in familiar rooms, where the echo of good times had ceased to resound."

'Twas a sunny day when eight-year-old Arne, along with his two brothers, three sisters, and parents packed up their families, ...packed up their family's most essential possessions, and left their home in Tallinn to escape escalating threats to the family's well-being from the occupying Russians.

---

19   Editor's Note: At the opening of one of his art shows, someone referred to Arne as a "Jewish artist." The comment seemed to unsettle him. By some measures, of course, he was Jewish—but growing up as a child during the Second World War had profoundly damaged his relationship with that identity. When I visited him at his home afterward, the encounter was still on his mind. It led us into a long conversation about the question, "What is a Jew?" From a very young age, Arne had been taught to hide his Jewishness so thoroughly that the word never felt like it could belong to him. His mother had warned him never to tell anyone—or even to speak the word—at any cost. Often, when Arne calls himself "un-German," what he is really saying is: Jewish.

Boarding a banana boat bound for Schwerin, Germany that usually hauled fruit from Africa, the Roosmans spent the next six days crossing the frigid ice-filled waters of the Baltic Sea.

They were fleeing the grip of one authoritarian dictator, just to land in the clutches of another dysfunctional demon with malevolent intentions.

Thinking back on how he felt as a child being forced to leave the only city he knew for reasons he did not understand, Arne reminisced about the voyage and bidding farewell to Tallinn.

"Vase of Flowers", *Axel Roosman*, watercolour on paper, 1949.

"Farewell", *Arne Roosman,* oil on canvas, 2014.

"A tearful farewell, from a place now turned as cold as the Siberia of the new masters. The ice, the icy Baltic Sea cooled my dream of captaining my own ship to distant shores. A strange world, the threatening, as well as reassuring sound of breaking ice. Thunder followed by invisible lightning. A crescendo, a whiplash, travelling at great speed into the icy darkness of the northern night. Our banana boat labours in two-quarter time with ice floes eating noisily at its hull... We were heading for the sunny coast of Poland, now a German protectorate. After two nights, stuck in the ice of the Bay of Riga, we were freed by the Soviet icebreaker Girmak.

This was possible while the Molotov/Ribbentrop Pact was still intact.

The ducks, oblivious to the goings-on, were enjoying the element.

The rest of us were worrying about bombs falling in the west, and the hammer and sickle dominating the east.

The glitter and military pomp. The musical welcome.

A marchy, trashy, never-seen-so-many-uniforms event."

– Arne Roosman

SNAPSHOTS OF UN-HUMANS

With little room to spare on the ship, Arne and his siblings had one toy — a doll named "Vanka Stanka" — to share between the six of them on the journey. Although there wasn't much room aboard for extra cargo, Arne said his parents brought with them a bunch of family photos. Some of the images were kept for their sentimental value, however, there were others they used as a passport of sorts. In these photographs, unlike the other cherished keepsakes, the faces of some of the individuals were missing; violently scratched out to send a message. Arne remembers his parents scratching the faces off anyone in their family photo albums who might garner the wrong sort of attention from any German or Russian troops they might encounter on their way. When questioned about the people in the photos by the authorities on either side, he said his parents would conveniently switch allegiances. If they were stopped by the Russians, the faceless people were affiliated with the Nazi scum. If they ran into the Nazis, the men without faces became 'Commie swine'.

"Roosman family and friends", circa approx. 1938.

"Roosman family and friends", circa approx. 1938.

The photograph featured the image of what appears to be a group of 10 friends posing in a comfortable and luxurious setting. While this could be the description of a photo found in anyone's family album, what distinguishes it as a significant artifact are the faces violently scratched off three of the 10 people.

"I was going through my notes the other day and I came across a bunch of photos I have taken for some of the articles I've written about you over the years. One image has been stuck in my brain. It's the one with a bunch of people's faces scratched out. You said your parents carried it with them during the war."

"When the Nazis saw the picture and said, 'Who are these people taken out?' Then my parents would say, 'Oh, they are Communists.' And if the Russians looked at the picture and said, 'Who are these people taken out?' They'd say, 'the Nazis.'"

"Wow, so they had to change their allegiance over and over just to survive. That must have been a shitty way to live. Especially with so many children to take care of."

"Whichever one you needed, you could say, because they were obliterated," said Arne. "There was no way that they could trace them. It would be too much of a chore to really find out who did it. That would be two years of FBI work. The photos were an easy alibi. Necessary lies."

"It's such a telling photograph! It really illustrates the fear one must experience as a refugee on the move during war time. It is hard to imagine how your parents must have felt when they had to pretend to be German one day, and then pretend to be Russian the next, switching their identity whenever necessary just to survive. Oh, yeah. Well, just for their own peace of mind, and to be left alone by the regional authorities."

"You saw the pictures of it sitting in the living room?" he asked.

"The one with all the faces scratched out?"

"Yeah, the one with my Auntie sitting on the Chesterfield with another woman. This someone who is sitting with her has her face scratched out, because she was a persona non grata.[20] With those several pictures, the photographs of their acquaintances, they took out acquaintances because either the Russians or the Nazis did not like them. That way, my parents could always say, 'well, they were bad people, so we took them out.'"

"So it was a way of covering your tracks?" I asked.

"That's right."

It rattled me the first time he showed me the photograph, because it spoke to the severity of the situation. We keep photos as mementos and reminders of the good times; in this case the Roosmans used them as a type of cloaking device to hide and shield them from any discrimination or hatred they may encounter during their immigration.

The photographs and Arne's experience of living through the Second World War as a child came up again in a conversation we had on November 2, 2021, for an article I was writing for *Bancroft This Week's* Remembrance Day edition. During our conversation, Arne described to me the horrific images etched in his mind from the war and its aftermath. It was the first time he shared with me how he still remembers the sounds of the bombs falling and seeing bloated corpses floating in the river. This was also the first time Arne opened up about what life was like for him and his family in Schwerin under the Nazis.

---

20   Editor's Note: These scratched out friends and family members would have been publicly known Jews or anti-fascists.

"Arne shares his photographs", *N. Smelle,* photograph, 2021.

"Axel's Schwerin", *Axel Roosman*, ink on paper, 1943.

A Foreigner In Schwerin

As I was leaving this place
Balancing on the potty, beats changing diapers.
Mum got hurt.
"There's blood on your leg."
Shnurry the cat locked up in the basement.
Sadly left behind when off to the Reich and the hidden Auschwitz;
for Axel preferable to the chance of an icy Siberia.
So, off to Deutschland!

They sing "Deutschland Uber Alles!", right there on the quay,
to welcome us and a bunch of other "un-Germans" to the law and order dictatorship.
The caning at school if you did not please Herr Waak with your abilities in mathematics.
Even after making Herr Mueller quite happy with his entrance in the morning.
A "true" Aryan, I suppose, blonde, and blue eyed,
"But Mum, what is a Jew?"

"Don't ask questions that get us into trouble, Arne," Helle replied.
Nazi youth one would see and hear on Sunday mornings, parading in the streets.
There was an annual outing to the country for children stuck in the urban city environment.
The kinderlandveshickung, where I spent some weeks in the Alps on the border of Switzerland.

– Arne Roosman

There is the great danger, and the great difference. France is a country, and Great Britain is several countries, but Italy is a man, Mussolini, and Germany is a man, Hitler. A man has ambitions, a man rules until he gets into economic trouble; he tries to get out of this trouble by war. A country never wants war until a man through the power of propaganda convinces it. Propaganda is stronger now than it has ever been before. Its agencies have been mechanized, multiplied, and controlled until, in a state ruled by any one man, truth can never be presented.
— Ernest Hemingway, 1935

Meeting in hurried conference at Brennero, on Italian soil, last week, Fuehrer Hitler of Germany and Duce Mussolini of Italy were believed to have discussed collaboration of economic interests in the present European set-up. The two dictators are shown, ABOVE, during Hitler's visit to Rome in 1938.

"Two Dictators hold historic conference in Brenner Pass", photo in *The Bancroft Times,* January 8, 1942.

"Back to School Again", *Arne Roosman*, oil on wood panel, 2021.

AN EDUCATION IN INDOCTRINATION

When I asked Arne about what life was like for him as a child living in Schwerin, Germany during the war, at the forefront of his mind was his experience as a student within the Nazis education system. The abundance of canings and overall brutality of his educational upbringing — a failed attempt by the Nazis to brainwash the young un-German — seems to have had the opposite effect on Arne's spirit than was intended by the Reich.

An average school day — like every school day under the Reich — began with the usual morning prayer, "Heil Hitler! Our Saviour Jesus Christ was not a Jew!" This was the greeting by Arne's teacher Herr Mueller every morning at the start of class. Hearing the same bullshit day after day made Arne wonder what his teacher was really saying.

"Well Nate, when I asked for clarification, I got a 'reasonable' answer," he said with a smirk. "He told me that not only was Jesus not a Jew. He was blue-eyed, blonde haired, and I assumed he must have spoken German. What was education like inside Hitler's Reich? Let's put it like this Nate, the caning was administered regularly by another, rather tall 'teacher', Herr Waak. He had lost a leg, an eye, and much of what we expected of a man in terms of civil behaviour. He surely enjoyed beating little boys on their tender behinds. The routine was as follows: we would start reading a chapter; soon after the reading began Waak would interrupt his evaluation; then, after the reading was finished, he would commandeer the Grade 5s and Grade 6s outside to be caned. One whack of the bamboo each. A constant victim, I found a way to protect myself by putting a book in my pants to absorb the blow. Herr Waak was hard of hearing as well, so he would not notice my creative pain management technique. But my hateful 'buddies' had to squeal. 'The bloody foreigner's cheating! That is what fucking foreigners do,' they would say. I have been some sort of a foreigner ever since, so it has become somewhat of a second nature."

At the end of most classes, for one reason or another, Arne found himself on the receiving end of Herr Waak's cane.

"One WHACK! of the bamboo," Arne said, slapping the table with both hands.

Education under the Nazis was mostly politically oriented, Arne explained. He said there was a strong emphasis on the "glory" of the German race and the "evil" nature of Hitler's convenient enemy, the Jew.

As a student in Schwerin, Arne remembers all too well what life during wartime was like for a child living in Germany during the Second World War. The sounds of gunfire, bombs raining down, watching corpses float by in the river: these types of gruesome encounters became a regular part of his day-to-day routine. Being immersed in such violence brought a swift end to the innocence of the Roosman children's childhood, Arne said.

Unimpressed with the Nazis' education system, Arne said he would look for any excuse he could to get out of class. According to Arne, his "wartime duties" provided the perfect reason. Although still a child, Arne was tasked with alerting the fire brigade after a bombing. If somehow the bomb did not ignite, he said his job was to grab the bomb and throw it back through the hole in the roof where it had entered. Frustrated with the daily washing of the brain ritual in the classroom, these duties, although dangerous and completely inappropriate for a child, provided a great reason to leave class. Fortunately, Schwerin avoided heavy bombardment thanks to the intervention of the Red Cross. Unfortunately, this made young Arne grow all too familiar with Herr Waak's cane.

"We got a few bombs, but they were sort of leftovers," said Arne. "Whenever the British fleets flew back home to England, they had to drop their bombs when they were up in the air. They couldn't land with their bombs, as it would be unsafe."

"Going over the recordings and notes from our interviews, I realized how throughout your life you have always been treated like a foreigner wherever you went. It must get exhausting."

"It becomes part of your existence. You're not anywhere. You are just an outsider, no matter where you turn. No matter where you are there is always somebody asking you where you're from. So, in a way I understand what it must be like for an African living in Canada or the U.S.A. who gets asked: 'Why are you here? In other words, why are you Black?' For me, it's 'why are you Estonian', or 'why did you come here'? What did you run away from?' It's a constant."

"Your experience as a young refugee, which seems to go hand in hand with forced immigration for people of all ages, is something that so many people around the world now can relate to. There are just so many people everywhere going through that today, right? Your story, what it must have felt like for you on that banana boat as a child, crossing the sea and seeing the ice and not really understanding where you are going and why your whole family is leaving your homeland must have been confusing for you and your brothers and sisters."

"It was just strange, because you could put it this way, there was a constant moving away from whatever direction the current was flowing... No matter where you move, your label that you don't belong is a constant, it's always there: 'oh yeah! I don't belong, no I don't, I don't belong.' And I've constantly been pushed into this kind of corner, 'Well, where are you from? Where are you from?' I looked like all those bloody Krauts ... and my grandmother was one, so that should make me belong, right? But it didn't. Bullying, there was plenty. The whole milieu of race, and such. We were all 'border people', like in the case of Estonians and Latvians, and especially their language, was considered of a lower class. Latvian, in German was Lettisch, rhymes with "Quatch", which in German means nonsense, and so on. There were a lot of rocks being thrown at each other as kids."

"You mentioned that you and your family were considered un-German. You weren't German enough at the beginning of the war, but then the Nazis needed more people power, so they loosened their definition of 'German.'"

"You were never enough, you know, for the dictators. It was the same with Stalin and the Ukrainians; he shipped 30 million people away to Siberia. They were the un-Russians."

"I've been hearing 'un-Canadian', and 'un-American' being tossed around."

"I could see why the Christian Canadian would think that the Muslim Canadian is un-Canadian," Arne said, "but what the Christian Canadian is forgetting is that they came, and they took away what was sacred to the Indigenous people here who were believing in the spirit of the trees, and the flowers, and the deer who eat them. These were God-like creatures. They didn't need to invent 'God', God is right here! It is the deer looking in my window."

"It's all sacred," I said.

"There is plenty of God right there," Arne replied.

Even though he was just a child of eight years old when he first experienced the bitter realities of life during wartime, the Reich's cruel curriculum of indoctrination did not sour his heart's ability to empathize and express compassion. Nor did it corrupt his soul with hatred or a passion for revenge. By mistake, the Nazis' intentional and institutional disregard for honesty and humanity, and the persistent heavy presence of the war looming way too close for comfort taught Arne Roosman to value peace.

"Back to School Again (Rough Draft)", *Arne Roosman,* pencil on paper, 2021.

The propagandist's purpose is to make one set of people forget that certain other sets of people are human.
– Aldous Huxley, 1937

"Nameless Faces", *Arne Roosman,* charcoal on paper, 1976.

AMERICAN NAZI INVASION

Hitler's promise of Lebensraum for all Germans demanded conquest. Throughout the 1930s the Nazi Party sowed seeds of hate in the U.S.A. by means of an organization called the German American Bund. At its peak the Bund had more than 100,000 members. Understanding that children were essential to the future of the Nazi movement, the Bund helped expand Hitler's fascist campaign in America by organizing summer camps for white, Christian, American kids.

With the intention of indoctrinating the next generation with Nazi propaganda — in a manner similar to that which Arne experienced under the Reich as a child and a student in Schwerin — the German American Bund would target children by removing them from "unhealthy city environments" and teaching them about nature, life skills, and why they should hate Jews, Blacks, socialists, communists, homosexuals, Gypsies, Catholics, and even Freemasons.

From its very core, the Bund, like Hitler and the Nazi government, was against the idea of democracy. Within the Reich, freedom of thought, speech and expression were not welcome.

As a Canadian, and someone who cherishes the relative freedom we enjoy here in North America, I have always assumed that the value of democracy was something that all of us, no matter our political stripes, could agree upon. Sadly, what far-right, ultra-nationalist movements such as the "Freedom" convoy and MAGA have shown us, is that for some, and tragically far too many, the hate-fueled flames of fascism are more comforting than a government for the people and by the people.

As Arne has pointed out to me more times than I can count, despite the violence it makes essential, there is an allure to fascism that seems to speak to those who have been convinced that the world is broken, and the dictator is the only one who can fix it.

This was clear on Feb. 20, 1939, when some 22,000+ American Nazis packed into New York's Madison Square Gardens to stand in solidarity with the Bund and Hitler's quest to expand the Reich worldwide. Preaching white supremacy under the guise of faux Patriotism, the Bund's primary objective — like that of Hitler, Mussolini, Putin, Trump and all other wannabe dictators around the globe — was to purify the nation of the "wrong people" to make it "Great Again" for the "right ones."

One of the main problems with fascism, aside from its inherently violent philosophy of might equals right, is that it grants almost absolute power to those in charge to decide who are the "wrong ones." As Martin Luther King Jr. told us, "The ultimate weakness of violence is that it is a descending spiral begetting the very thing it seeks to destroy; instead of diminishing evil, it multiplies it. Through violence you may murder the liar, but you cannot murder the lie, nor establish the truth. Through violence you may murder the hater, but you do not murder hate. In fact, violence merely increases hate. Returning violence for violence multiplies violence, adding deeper darkness to a night already devoid of stars. Darkness cannot drive out darkness; only light can do that. Hate cannot drive out hate; only love can do that" (King Jr. 1967).

Although the number of Nazis in America had grown significantly, the number of anti-fascists fighting for freedom at home and abroad was growing even faster. Journalist Dorothy Thompson, the first foreign correspondent kicked out of Germany when Hitler took power, attended the rally that night in protest of the hate that the Nazis were spreading. She caught onto what Hitler was up to early and wasn't afraid to tell people about his plan. Surrounded by the 22,000+ Nazis assembled there that evening, Thompson reportedly disrupted the rally, laughing and shouting during the speeches.

Eventually, for her own safety, she had to be rescued by police and escorted out of the building. Outside of the Gardens cheering for Thompson while waiting for attendees after the rally, were about 100,000 angry anti-fascists, looking for a Nazi to slap.

"A Face With No Name", *Arne Roosman*, charcoal on paper, 2005.

NOTE THESE IMPORTANT FACTS

ABOUT YOUR

NEW RATION BOOK

.. to Save Yourself Trouble

The new Ration Books No. 1, now being distributed, do NOT become valid and must not be used until Monday, September 7th, 1942. They will be good for the six months period commencing September 7th.

DATES ON WHICH TEA, COFFEE AND SUGAR COUPONS BECOME VALID

COUPONS NOS. 1 and 2: are valid September 7th, 1942 and thereafter
COUPONS NOS. 3 and 4: are valid October 5th, 1942 and thereafter
COUPONS NOS. 5 and 6: are valid November 2nd, 1942 and thereafter
COUPONS NOS. 7 and 8: are valid November 30th, 1942 and thereafter
COUPONS NOS. 9 and 10: are valid December 28th, 1942 and thereafter
COUPONS NOS. 11 and 12: are valid January 25th, 1943 and thereafter
COUPON NO. 13: is valid February 22nd, 1943 and thereafter

Each coupon is good for a two weeks' ration, and two coupons may be used at a time to buy a supply for four weeks.

● **SUGAR COUPONS:** The red coupons, imprinted with the word 'Sugar'—the first page of coupons in the book—are the only ones to be used for sugar, and they are to be used for sugar only. Each coupon is good for a two weeks' ration; that is, one pound of sugar.

● **TEA AND COFFEE COUPONS:** The green coupons — the second page of coupons in the book—although marked 'Spare A'— are to be used for tea and/or coffee. Each coupon is good for a two weeks' ration of either tea OR coffee; that is, two ounces of tea OR eight ounces of coffee. Only the green coupons can be used for tea or coffee.

● **OTHER COUPONS:** There are three other series of coupons in the book, namely 'Spare B', 'Spare C', and 'Spare D'. No use for these coupons has been designated. Do not detach these coupons from your book.

DO NOT USE DETACHABLE POSTCARD NOW

The detachable return postcard at the back of the new Ration Book is intended for use when applying for your Ration Book No. 2. If this postcard is lost or used improperly, there may be complications and delays when the time comes to get the next book. DO NOT USE THE DETACHABLE POSTCARD UNTIL YOU ARE ADVISED TO DO SO.

You must write your name and address in ink in the space provided at the top of each sheet of coupons—and you must write the serial number of your book in the space provided on the stub at the side of each sheet of coupons.

All coupons must be detached in the presence of the storekeeper. It is illegal for him to accept loose coupons.

Penalties are provided for improper use of Ration Books.

The inside front cover of your Ration Book shows the location of your nearest Ration office. Your enquiries should be addressed to that office. Always give serial number of your Ration Book when writing.

THE WARTIME PRICES AND TRADE BOARD

OTTAWA

W.P. 8

"Note These Important Facts About Your New Rations Book to Save Yourself Trouble", The Wartime Prices and Trade Board, in *The Bancroft Times*, 1940.

THE ART OF RATIONING

To aid in the war effort, strict conservation measures were enacted in Canada in 1940, which saw government restrictions of the public's consumption of: gasoline, sugar, coffee, tea, butter, and a wide range of other food products and household supplies.

The headline on the front page of the December 18, 1940 edition of The Bancroft Times read "Gas Ration, Quarterly Basis: No Hoarding Coupons From One Period to Next."

Informing the public then and now about the many sacrifices made by Canadians in the name of the Allies' fight for democracy, the article stated:

> Gasoline rationing will be on a quarterly basis, it was learned Monday. Under the plan, which munitions minister Howe announced last week would go into effect April 1, motorists will be allowed to save coupons, but we will be required to use them in a specific three-month period, it is understood. The coupons will be issued for a year but will be divided into quarters to expire June 30, September 30, December 31, and March 31. The adoption of such a plan will prevent motorists from saving their winter coupon quota for use in summer months. The amount of gasoline motorists are likely to receive is not expected to be announced until shortly before the rationing becomes effective and will depend on the available supply at the time.
> –The Bancroft Times, 1940

EFFECTIVE NOW

TEA and COFFEE

are rationed by coupon

The ration is one ounce of tea or four
ounces of coffee per person, per week

Coupons A, B, C, D, and E, on the Temporary War
Ration Card, now in the hands of the public, are to be
used, and are NOW valid for the purchase of tea
and coffee.

Each coupon will entitle the purchaser to one ounce of
tea or four ounces of coffee - a supply for one week.

If desired, purchasers may use any or all of these five
coupons simultaneously, and buy up to 5 weeks supply
at one time, on the surrender of the appropriate number
of coupons.

Numbered coupons are good only for the purchase of
sugar and may not be used to buy tea or coffee.
Similarly, lettered coupons may not be used to buy
sugar.

**COFFEE CONCENTRATES AND
SUBSTITUTES CONTAINING
COFFEE**

One coupon must be surrendered for
each quantity of coffee concentrate
or substitute containing coffee, suf-
ficient to make 12 cups of beverage.

**TEA BAGS REQUIRE
COUPONS**

When purchasing tea bags, the following coupon values shall be used:

1 coupon for a carton of 12 or 20 tea bags
4 coupons for a carton of 48 or 60 tea bags
1 coupon for a carton of 15 tea bags.

CHILDREN UNDER 12 YEARS OF AGE ARE NOT
ELIGIBLE TO RECEIVE ANY RATION OF TEA OR COFFEE.

SPECIAL NOTICE TO RETAILERS

On and after August 3rd, retailers must establish
their right to purchase new supplies of tea or
coffee from their suppliers by turning over to the
supplier currently valid ration coupons,
equivalent to the poundage of tea or
coffee ordered from the supplier

THE WARTIME PRICES AND TRADE BOARD

Ottawa, August 3rd, 1942.

"Effective Now: Tea and Coffee are Rationed by Coupon", The Wartime
Prices and Trade Board, in *The Bancroft Times*, 1942.

That same week, to help keep the war machine rolling ahead, Canada's Federal Munitions Minister Clarence Decatu Howe also banned the sale of new tires. Imagine asking North Americans today to make such a sacrifice.

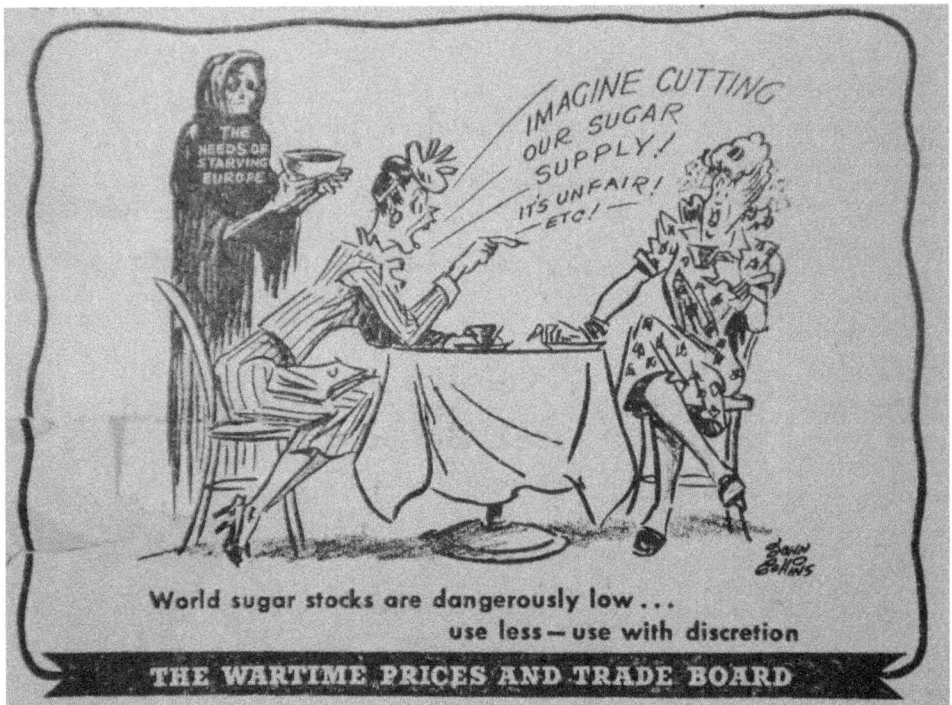

"The Wartime Prices and Trade Board", Ad in *The Bancroft Times,* August 16, 1945.

"Jungle Book", *Arne Roosman*, oil on canvas, 2014.

Whenever and wherever men have engaged in the mindless slaughter of animals (including other men), they have often attempted to justify their acts by attributing the most vicious or revolting qualities to those they would destroy; and the less reason there is for the slaughter, the greater the campaign of vilification.
– Farley Mowat, 2000

THE LAST DAY AT THE ZOO

As the war continued consuming the lives of the innocent and guilty, Mother Nature was busy doing her usual thing: making everything grow. There was an abundance of mushrooms of many edible varieties growing in the forests around Schwerin. Every Autumn Arne's Uncle Richard traveled from Berlin in his Ford Model 'T' to help Axel with the harvest and assist his niece Helle with the pickling and preserving. Considering most families did not have a car in those days, Uncle Richard's visits were always an exciting time for the Roosmans.

According to Arne, Uncle Richard was a strange, quiet man, with many "mysterious" ties to power on all sides of the war. In peacetime, he said his uncle was an officer of the Tsarist Navy in Estonia, and chief of a large English insurance company. During the war, Richard lived in Hitler's Berlin, along with his Russian wife and one daughter, who confessed to him that she wanted to marry a Spanish crowned prince and move to Spain. Arne said Hitler's chief propogandist, Joseph Goebbles, told his cousin, "No, not unless you settle in Deutschland."

When the war ended, Richard took his family to the U.S.A., where Arne said they made Oklahoma their new home. Although Richard's daughter would never get her happily ever after with a Spanish prince, she did marry a man who was a Colonel in the U.S. Armed Forces, and a cousin of Mamie Eisenhower. They started a business looking after old people, strange people. In war and at peace, Arne and his siblings always wondered if their Uncle Richard was secretly a spy.

172

"Our dear uncle deserves some attention," said Arne. "He was an officer in the Navy of Tsar Nicholas II of Russia when back home in Estonia with his beautiful Russian wife. In charge of international businesses in Hitler's Reich during the war, he was also promptly associated with U.S.A. Allies. A man of mysterious connections whom Axel with his young trio visited in his swank apartment in Berlin the day before the night the Allies bombed the zoo. With all the creatures running amok, our three plus one, well on our way to 'safe' Schwerin."

"Well, we were there on that day visiting Berlin and our relatives who lived there. Our Uncle Richard lived close to the zoo, so of course daddy took his three sons to the zoo to see all the animals. We took the afternoon train back to Schwerin. En route the train was stopped – because they stopped the trains whenever there were planes up in the air bombing. That was the first major hit on Berlin and the zoo by the Allies on that particular day in 1943. We were halfway home to Schwerin, and there were 800,000 Allied planes up in the air, bombing and dropping their excess bombs, because they could not land with all the bombs that they didn't drop. They couldn't take them back to England, to London, or wherever because they were a hazard at landing. They dropped them en route over Germany, Poland, wherever, so that they were empty when they landed. Those bombs were dropped around the very train that we were on. The trains were all in the dark because they didn't have any lights on. That way the guys in the air wouldn't even see the train on the ground. If they had seen us, they would have been more accurate, and we would have all been dead. We would have been the target because we were in the way of the bombs."

"You must have been terrified."

"Well," Arne said, "we were just sitting in the train, waiting. You're waiting to be released by whoever was in charge to say, 'OK, this train can move on.'"

"So what happened when they dropped the bombs on Berlin? What happened at the zoo? Did the animals escape? A lot must have been killed."

"Yeah, many of them. Berlin was the target, and the Allies

didn't really give a shit whether they hit Hitler on the head, or they hit a tiger on the head. No, they were hitting Berlin."

"The Wolf at the Window", *Arne Roosman,* charcoal on paper, 2014.

"Hitler's not going to teach my children!" Ad in *The Bancroft Times,* May 28, 1942.

"Herr Waak/May the Bugs Get His Wooden Leg",
Arne Roosman, mixed media on paper, 2014.

*Coming of age in a fascist police state will not be a barrel of fun for anybody,
much less for people like me, who are not inclined to suffer Nazis gladly,
and feel only contempt for the cowardly flag suckers,
who would gladly give up their outdated freedom to live for the mess of pottage they have
been conned into believing will be freedom from fear.*
– Hunter S. Thompson, 2003

RATS, SQUEALERS, AND THE FOREVER FOREIGNER

School for a young Un-German boy under the Nazis wasn't easy. Bombarded with a barrage of misinformation intended to brainwash the next generation into worshipping and eventually sacrificing themselves for Hitler's dream of world domination, Arne's curiosity, open mind, and gentle soul were tested daily by heavy-handed teachers and schoolyard bullies. Enjoying lunch at The Granite restaurant in Bancroft on March 20th, 2024, he explained to me what it was like enduring the Third Reich's indoctrination as a child.

"Squealing seemed to be a German kind of thing," Arne told me. "The local Germans considered us foreigners — newcomers — so they were always somehow 'superior' to us. The students would always be looking over my shoulder when I was drawing, and their comment would inevitably be, 'Wow! These foreigners really know how to draw!' Sort of a positive and a negative because they said it out of jealousy."

"These were the Nazis' kids?" I asked.

"Well, I wouldn't call them Nazi kids," Arne clarified. "Some of their parents were actually communists, because in Germany communism was very entrenched at the time."

"So they were the children of Nazis and Communists. That must have been fun."

"Oh yeah! There was a lot of bullying!"

Despite the daily trauma of war, Arne found moments of light within the darkness, as a curious child so full of life and dreams. When I asked Arne about what it was like going through puberty in Germany during the war, he said there was one student that made him not want to practice social distancing. Her name was Agnes, and she was Arne's first crush. The next time I stopped by to visit, he handed me this note about his childhood sweetheart.

I was nine years old, or younger, so was Agnes and likely everyone else. First year students all versant in our skills, be it at language, math, and lots of uncalled for extracurricular, let's have a fun sort of attitude. And there is Agnes. Her name is close to the spelling of the angel, which she was in my eyes, elevated beyond the clouds, floating in the sky. Blue, her eyes, under the most unusual stretch of a dark blackish eyebrow uninterrupted, separates the eyes, nose, and lovely lips from the strawberry locks, so typical of Estonian looks...

Imagine this youthful infatuation reminded some 70 years later, seeing a spitting image of Agnes with her so personal eyebrow, and the blonde with the black from the blue, in a restaurant in Toronto. My intent, the next time I saw her in this neighbourhood eatery was to approach her and query whether she might be the granddaughter of my dreams [Agnes]. However frequently I dropped by the local, she never did show up.
– Arne Roosman, 2024

"Arne", *Axel Roosman,* pencil on paper, 1941.

THROUGH THE EYES OF A CHILD

At 10 years old, Arne found himself at the winter resort of Sibratsgfäll in the western alps of Austria, which were now part of Hitler's Reich. He spent several weeks at the resort. He said it was customary in the Reich to send children from cities in both the summer and winter on vacations to the lovely countryside.

On one of these class trips during the winter, Arne got a kick in the ass by Mother Nature when downhill skiing with a group of his friends.

"A group of us went on an afternoon ski trip. We were just kids, skillful enough by now to be let loose on the mountainside."

As Arne attempted to navigate the steep slope on the banks of the creek, he said his left ski shook loose from its binding and disappeared down the mountain and out of sight. Exhausting as it was for him to limp down the mountain on one ski, he said looking back on that day always brings him a smile.

The reason for these school field trips into the Alps was two-fold, Arne told me. Of course, on the one hand they were intended to relieve the students from the stress of life in the city during the war. However, more importantly, Arne said, was that they wanted to show the children that their "Fatherland" was something worth fighting for once they were old enough to join the military.

"It was a kind of propaganda," he explained. "They took us

there to give us a break from the city, and the war, and all that. But what they really wanted was to show us how beautiful Germany is, so that when we were old enough, we would join the war machine. They were always shipping the city kids out from the cities in the summer and winter, because cities got bombed, and all the young people were future soldiers to die for Hitler," explained Arne. "They did not want them to be bombed by the Allies before they were 15."

"Why 15?"

"Because at 15 you went to war to save the Reich or expand it."

"You must have been close to being sent off to war?"

"Well, my older brother turned 14 in November of 1944, so we were really worried. If the war lasted one more year, then my brother Gus would have had to go into the army. Because by that time the army was taking everybody over the age of 15. There were guys that were 89-years-old, and they were all dressed in old uniforms, because they weren't making new uniforms anymore."

"Why did the Nazis stop making uniforms?"

"They managed to kill around six million Jews," he explained, "but to kill six million Jews they had to do some sacrificing of their own. They had to sacrifice their own boys, and around two million of them died on the Russian front. So there was no one to make the uniforms because everyone had to join the army, even my Dad got pulled into the war."

No sunny peace can wash away
the imprint of horror of the incessant bombing.
My soul is crying for no more war,
but the porridge is too thick to swallow.
– Arne Roosman

"HEIL dem teufel!", *Arne Roosman*, charcoal and conte on paper, 2023.

AXEL GOES TO ITALY

The war was nearing its end by the time Arne's father Axel was yanked into the Nazi war machine. Until then, Axel had avoided being drafted into the war effort, because of his age and the fact that he had seven children to care and provide for. However, as the war was nearing its end and the Nazi regime was falling apart, Axel was sent to Northern Italy to manage a work facility that was manufacturing barricades meant to keep the Allies at bay. When Axel arrived at the facility, Arne said he was told that the Italian partisans living in the forest nearby would kill him. To stay alive, a friend of his in the village recommended that he feed the resistance by sharing the provisions sent by the Nazis for the workers with the partisans.

I asked Arne about Axel's time in Italy while seated in his backyard one afternoon in late July 2022.

"My Dad was previously not taken into the army because he had us seven kids that he was responsible for," Arne said. "He also had a trade that was very helpful for the average community – he was working as a surveyor, measuring distances and had his own surveying department – so he was needed. But then of course, near the end of the war they only needed people at the front. Because he

"No HEIL, all kaput!", *Arne Roosman*, charcoal and conte on paper, 2023.

was now 45-years-old, he was not given guns and rifles; he was put in charge of managing the building of concrete barricades around the coast to prevent the Allies from landing."

By the time his father was sent to Italy, Arne said the Allies had already landed in Sicily and were fighting their way up the Italian boot. In the wake of Mussolini's arrest and dismissal, Italy's King Victor Emmanuel III appointed Marshal Pietro Badoglio as the deposed dictator's replacement. Only amid the lunacy of war could replacing a fascist dictator with a war criminal like Badoglio – the man who ordered the use of Mustard Gas on Ethiopian civilians during the Italian invasion – be considered a step in the right direction.

Nonetheless, seeing the writing on the wall after taking over as Italy's Prime Minister, Badoglio was more than happy to turn his back on the Nazis when he joined forces with the Allies, Arne said.

"Il Duce's guys, the fascisti we're now out of power," explained Arne. "The communists, and the left — the anti-Nazis and anti-fascists — had taken over."

This was the context of chaos which welcomed Arne's father Axel when he arrived in Italy. Upon his arrival, Arne said he was told by the locals that he would be dead within three months in his current role with the Reich. When Axel asked why he would not survive beyond the next three months, Arne said he was told by some of the townspeople, "Look, the partisans will kill you. They kill a German camp commandant every three months."

Questioning what he could do to save his skin, they told Axel, "Well, you can't do anything. You're a fucking German and we are Italian Communists. We have had enough of the fascisti. Hitler, Mussolini, you name it, we don't want it."

"Jesus! It's a miracle he survived."

"Well, he was only there for about six months, but he did what he had to, to survive."

Understanding the danger he was in, Arne said his Dad had to ask himself, "How do I survive, because in three months I'll be dead?"

With few options, none good, Arne told me that a woman

Axel had befriended said his best chance of surviving was to feed the Communist partisans with the rations meant for the German workers at the facility he managed. Although if caught he would end up in a concentration camp such as Birkenhaus or Auschwitz, Arne said Axel decided to take his chances by supplying the Communists and the partisans with what they needed.

"Dad thought, 'If the Germans discover that I'm a traitor, they'd send me to outfits because I'm also a foreigner — and Estonian — so they probably won't just shoot me right away. They'll likely send me to the gas chambers.' That seemed to be the technique."

Arne said the partisans would come in from the forest during the daytime to work on building the barricades at the facility Axel managed, and then they would disappear into the mountains and continue "doing their good/bad thing."

At this stage, Arne said the Italians did not have a regular army anymore, except for the one that had been fighting in Ukraine for Germany until the fascist power structure disintegrated when Mussolini was killed.

"With Mussolini disappearing," explained Arne, "the political situation in Italy changed. It was strictly nobody's country. There were two powerful combatants — the Nazis and the Allies — fighting in a territory that was only semi administered by the communist managers in charge. Eventually, when the conflict was over, and the Nazis and the Americans got out of there, those people took over... the ones that were partisans. Of course, a lot of the elite Italians left, and the anti-fascist bureaucracy, or Inteligencia, they were all waiting to clean up the country. Once all those foreigners were out, the bad guys, the Krauts, the good guys, the Allies, then the partisans could do their own thing again. Those were the powers that were waiting on the sidelines, while the Allies were chasing out the Nazis, and Daddy was stuck in the middle, trying not to be German."

"Daddy would say, 'Don't kill me, and I'll get you salami.' My dad was not a Nazi, but they didn't know that. To them the important thing was what he was doing there. He was making

"No Demi-Gods Allowed!", *Arne Roosman,* charcoal and conte on paper, 2023.

barricades to keep the liberators away."

Of course, immediately this would have put Axel on the wrong side of the partisans who were eager to dismantle the Nazi regime. So, according to Arne, Axel would tell them, "Look you guys, I'm not really trying to keep the liberators away. I'm only stuck in my job, and if I don't do this job, they put me in Auschwitz, in a gas chamber. Now are you going to shoot me because I'm trying not to end up in a gas chamber? Or, do you want me to get you more salami, and all these goodies?"

"Where did he get all of the food and supplies from?"

"The Germans were still occupying Italy, you see. So, they were feeding the Italians, because they were in charge of the economy. Daddy Roosman, who is in charge of this camp, he had around 200 Italian workers working on those pyramids [barricades], they all had to be fed. They were legitimate workers for the German army, and the German army didn't give a shit whether they were communist or partisan. To them, each worker was a worker. When he would go home, and en route, kill a German guard, they don't know. They don't see that because these guys live in the woods. to the Krauts, they are workers that put up concrete barriers to stop the allies. If they kill those workers, then the Allies will kill more Germans. So the Germans had to be careful how many workers they killed or considered partisans. Because each time they did away with a partisan who they thought was a bad guy, another American, English, or Canadian gets away and is able to kill a Kraut... so it was like a chess game, where everyone is deciding which move to make, and which move would get you killed. none of them gave a shit about dad, except the partisans because they got the salami."

"Incredible! So, in a way, salami saved your Dad's life."

"Ho, ho, I guess that's true," he laughed, before polishing off his beer.

"So as long as he was bringing them the salami, they'd let him live. Wow!"

"Daddy didn't give them the bullets. The bullets came from the Krauts, and the Krauts got bullets from the Allies, and Dad is caught in between. If he didn't give them the salami, he'd get a bullet too."

"What a nightmare!"

Axel managed to survive in Italy for almost six months, however, because he was suffering from severe arthritis, he was sent to Grock's Castle in the Italian Alps to recover before he was sent back to Schwerin to reunite with his family. Fortunately for the Roosmans, Axel was home in time to experience the end of the war with his family.

While Axel reunited with his family, Mussolini and Petacci were attempting to flee to Switzerland, where they planned to escape by plane to Spain. The two along with their entourage – mostly consisting of Mussolini's former ministers – were stopped near the village of Dongo near Lake Como on April 27, 1945. While various accounts of the execution differ in minor details – some of which proclaimed that Mussolini behaved like a coward in his final moments – all of them acknowledged that at 4:10 p.m., he, along with Petacci and several of his ministers that had been travelling with them on the train, were lined up against an exterior wall of the Villa Belmonte, and shot with a submachine gun. In the early hours of the next day, the corpses of Mussolini, Petacci and the other fascists were loaded into a vehicle and transported to Milan. There, the bodies were hung upside down from the roof of an Esso gas station in the old Piazzale Loreto.

"Arne Roosman in his early teens, left, along with his younger brother Benny", photograph, circa approx. 1946.

"A Divided World", *Arne Roosman,* mixed media on paper, 2021.

The first casualty, when war comes, is truth.
– Hiram Johnson, 1918

MORE GOOD NEWS

Inside Germany during the war, Arne said it was often very difficult to discern the difference between accurate information and misinformation, because the Nazis used propaganda as a weapon against the Allies and their own people so effectively. He said sometimes they would find out important news on the same day something big happened, but most of the time they had to wait days or longer to find out what was going on outside their bubble in Schwerin.

"It would depend on who was giving the information," he said. "It could have come from Berlin, Switzerland; Austria was right there, so there were all these communications. It was total chaos! When you look at the maps of the war years, for a General to make a decision to do this or do that, they were all off track. They didn't know what they were doing."

The Nazis' misinformation campaigns were in many ways successful in terms of brainwashing the German people, and garnering support for Hitler. However, many Germans realized they had been duped by their leader, when the truth of Hitler's death came out.

In big bold 200 pt font, on the front page of the Wednesday, May 2, 1945 Paris edition of The Stars and Stripes newspaper — the "Daily Newspaper of U.S. Armed Forces" in Europe — were the words the majority of the world were praying to hear: "HITLER DEAD."

The German radio announced last night that Adolf Hitler had died yesterday afternoon, and that Adm. Doenitz, former commander-in-chief of the German Navy, had succeeded him as ruler of the Reich. The Stars and Stripes reported that Doenitz, speaking later over the German radio, declared that "Hitler has fallen at his command post. My first task is to save the German people from destruction by Bolshevism. If only for this task, the struggle will continue." The announcement preceding the proclamation by Doenitz said: "It is reported from the Fuehrer's headquarters that our Fuehrer, Adolf Hitler, has fallen this afternoon at his command post in the Reich Chancellery, fighting to the last breath against Bolshevism and for his country. On April 30, the Fuehrer appointed Grand Adm. Doenitz as his successor. The new Fuehrer will speak to the German people... Doenitz said: 'German men and women, soldiers of the German Wehrmacht, our Fuehrer, Adolf Hitler has fallen. German people are in deepest mourning and veneration. Adolf Hitler recognized beforehand the terrible danger of Bolshevism and devoted his life to fighting it. At the end of this, his battle, and his unswerving straight path of life, stands his death as a hero in the capital of the Reich. All his life meant service to the German people. His battle against the Bolshevik flood benefited not only Europe but the whole world. The Fuehrer has appointed me as his successor. Fully conscious of the responsibility, I take over the leadership of the German people.'
- *The Stars and Stripes*, 1945

Page one of New York's Daily News declared, "NAZI RADIO ANNOUNCES: HITLER DEAD 'FELL IN COMMAND POST' ADMIN. DOENITZ NAMED HEAD OF REICH, ARMY." By the next day, the front page of the Daily Express in London announced, "LATEST: SUICIDE BY HITLER, GOEBBELS." Above the main headline another statement in smaller bold font: "BERLIN FALLS

AND 1,000,000 SURRENDER IN ITALY: Dramatic news last night points to early end of Nazi's phony war."

As stated in The Stars and Stripes article, the news actually broke a day early on German radio when it was announced that Hitler had died in battle. Immediately after reports of Hitler's death were broadcast on May 1, 1945, Arne said a woman's voice could be heard echoing through the streets of Schwerin. She was shouting: "Der Anführer ist tot! Der Anführer ist tot!" Not all Germans shared the woman's enthusiasm for the death of their dictator. The woman's celebration was tragically cut short, Arne said, when a small gang of Nazi Youth thugs heard her joyful proclamation and strung her up by the neck from a lamp post for all to see.

"The hanging woman, in a way, she's really important because it shows the brutality of how people were treated by the Nazis," Arne said. "Here is a German woman – not an un-German woman, the real thing – and she just didn't like the politics of Hitler."

"So these Nazi teenagers killed her because they didn't like what she had to say. And these kinds of pricks are still people flying the Nazi flag today, even here in Canada! Where did they kill her?"

"She was just a few blocks down from the pond in the middle of Schwerin."

"So close to home," I said, trying to imagine what it must have been like to witness such horror as a child.

"What is important to remember is that when Hitler committed suicide," explained Arne, "we who lived in Germany were not told that he committed suicide. Hitler died. He just died. That's what we were told because it would have been a bad mark on the 'Leader' for being such a shit-face that he couldn't take defeat, so he killed himself and his wife Eva Braun. This 'saintly hero' figure, Adolf Hitler, suddenly he was an un-hero."

"A Woman Hung/The Day the Freak Kills the Freak", *Arne Roosman*, mixed media on paper, 2019.

"Yeah, that's what you said, 'real German heroes don't kill themselves; they go down in battle'."

"That's right, they face the enemy, and they shoot; and if they get shot, well, they're like Christ. He was up on the cross, he didn't run away ... he faced the music. So, Hitler and Christ, were in the minds of his followers, the same kind of guy."

"So, Hitler was their messiah; like Trump is to the MAGA cult."

"Yeah, it's not that different. You know, deep down the people that are pro-Trump, and others that approve of what he's doing, forgive his every misstep. Because good guys don't make any missteps. Trump has done nothing wrong in their minds. And people claim that journalists are lying about him, right? When really, it's him lying about himself."

"He's always the victim," I said. "All his problems are everyone else's fault. He's always 'sacrificing' himself for the people, 'his people'."

"I don't remember much of that day, except the horror of the hanging body, dripping piss," Arne said. "And that it was a sunny day. They didn't say anything about Hitler committing suicide. That was kept top secret for a while because as you know, German heroes don't commit suicide; they face their enemy or adversary. See, in a way this is where the myth of Hitler being one of these strong men collapses. He was trying to get into Valhalla, but Odin and these bums are telling him 'Look, demi-gods don't get in here!' When he committed suicide his illusion of glory fell apart. So heroes don't commit suicide, but some pathetic wannabe demigods do."

"A lot of his high-ranking officers killed themselves as well," I said.

"Yeah, they knew they were history, and most of them committed suicide. Göring killed himself. His wife gave him some pills in prison. He was in Nuremberg having a trial, when the verdict was announced that they were all going to be hung by the neck. The German naval officer Alwin-Broder Albrecht – the Nazis' 'King of the Sea' – is also believed to have committed suicide. His body was never found though. Of course, Hitler's suicide was never on the news, because when a 'superhero' dies, they do not commit suicide. It's that simple. It's a sentimental kind of thing, so they made sure the population didn't know. Of course you can't stop rumours, so it only took a day or two for the news of his suicide spread across the country. People are constantly yapping. We want to know, and we want to tell you."

"Allies have liberated dozen European Capitals", *The Bancroft Times*,
November 9, 1944.

"Liberation Day/Childhood's End", *Arne Roosman,* mixed media on paper, 2014.

End of War,
Begins Peace
Gods colourful cathedrals, walls, and museums,
Nazi Christ,
Blue-eyed lies.
The people's Universe of Supreme masculinity.
All the way a teen, staggering, in No Man's, No Woman's, No Halos land
to enlighten Darwinian concepts.
–Arne Roosman

A LIGHT IN THE DARKNESS

Less than a week after Hitler's death was announced, the Nazis unconditionally surrendered, signing the papers early in the morning hours of May 7, 1945. A few weeks later, the Roosmans' world would fundamentally change again when the Allied troops arrived in Schwerin. It wasn't the "Liberators" who showed up in Schwerin first after Germany's surrender though. Instead, it was the "Liberated" who came knocking on doors and windows in search of food, water, and clothing. Arne lamented on his midnight visitors in his book A *"Touch Of Arsenic: Sketching the Past"*.

The young polyglot is a little boy no more, and will have to acquire the new language of the defeated,
and the new currency, excuses, feeble explanation.
I'll have to sort out the altogether new grammar.
The liberators come in skirts.
They come in jeeps operated with one foot, and glove compartments,
full of goodies for thieving locals.
The plunder from the freight chains will bake bread and feed daddy's hungry hoard.
A deadly blow from the last good German will kill the thief of the boots from the trunk of a refugee.
The darkness speaks to my window.
The darkness asks for my dead grandpa's suit, a shirt,
anything with no stripes.
The stripes will adorn the pavement in the morning.
Oh, bugs of casual childhood, cry!
— **Arne Roosman**

CHILDHOOD'S END

Tired of the war, and the killing, and being un-German, Arne and his family welcomed the Allies. This caused problems for him and his brothers with some of the "real" German kids in their neighbourhood.

"There were all sorts of these kind of situations in our neighborhood in Schwerin," Arne said. "When the Allies came in, the Germans had lost the war, and since me and my brothers were always called un-German, we were happy to see them. So, if you talked to a lot of the neighborhood kids, well, they called me and my brothers' traitors. They said, 'Now you're turning your cape in the wind.' Because the Nazis were defeated, Germany has been defeated, suddenly they accused me of being pro-America. Well, you made me un-German? So what is your problem with me being pro-American because I'm not German enough anyway."

"You couldn't win, Arne."

"If someone called them the liberators, they would say, 'liberators of what?'"

"The liberators of the un-Germans!"

"So that's what I ran into with the neighbourhood cronies. See if you live in the neighborhood for three years, inevitably, some of the people become very closely acquainted because you see them every day, right? You go to school together and you see these kids your same age, 12-year-olds, and when you were an un-German, you were seen as a sort of trash. Suddenly the un-German is pro-American, so now we were bad guys. Then you were a traitor, because you lived under Hitler for three or four years, and now you were denying Hitler. You were just not in with the neighbourhood boys anymore. Yeah. Your buddies were now gone because to them you were traitors to the fatherland."

"Well, in that case it wasn't a bad thing if you didn't have the Reich stuff, Arne."

"You are a German, and you are a traitor because you're with the Americans. That's what they would say. I was never against the Americans the way you were, I would say. You made the war. I was running away from the bloody Russians with their war idea. We were running away from wars ... and there were wars all around us."

"Being in that situation as a kid must have been brutal," I said. "I can see now what you were talking about before, when you said you always felt like a foreigner. How could you not when you're living there, trying to get away from the Russians? Then you get there, and they call you 'un-German!' Then the Allies come in and liberate the country, give Hitler and the Nazis the boot, and you're still a traitor. It's like, what the hell do you want from me? That's a lot to deal with as an adult, let alone when you're a kid."

"Axel's Currency", 50 Krooni, 1929.

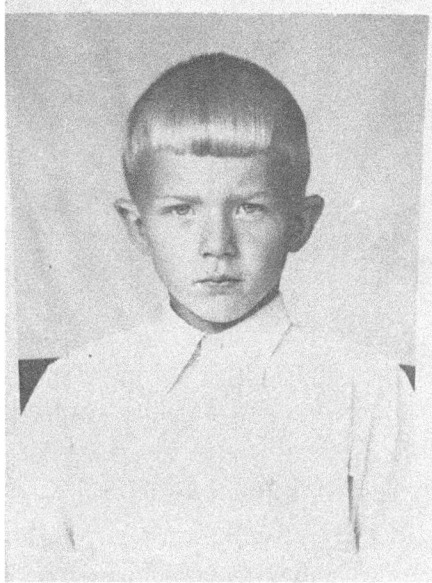

"9 Year Old Arne Roosman", photograph, 1941.

Racing around a fenced-in DP camp.
In our early teens, and in superb shape.
Exploring three kilometres of Göring's private hunting grounds.
Pea soup, pea bread for weeks.
Then switch to cornbread and corn soup.
Boils popping up here, and there, and everywhere on our bodies.
Our liberators felt unappreciated, so they put us on local German rations.
Black rye bread, and other spartan-inspired cookery from the Volxkuche,
the people's leftovers.
Fresh fruit was never out of reach of the local farmers who pruned the
roadside orchards well.
– Arne Roosman

DISPLACED AND DISPOSABLE

There I was, strolling along the edge atop of the Eagle's Nest in Bancroft. Panting in the heat of the late summer, tanning my tongue in sunshine, I was thinking of my last visit with Arne and everything he had shared with me about life in the DP camps after the war was over. "Did it ever really end?" I pondered as I paused to admire the view of the vast expanses of forests below.

Getting comfortable on a boulder just off the beaten path, I decided to go over my notes from our conversation the previous week. Spreading them out on the rock and weighing them down with some of the sticks and stones nearby, I began organizing them into a timeline. And in a way, that has been the purpose of sharing Arne's story together in this book; to establish a timeline tracing his steps through history from now backwards.

My intention in putting pieces of his personal puzzle together in these pages: to, as the freedom fighter Ida B. Wells-Barnett said, "turn the light of truth upon" the malevolent forces so hell-bent on raping the planet and exploiting any person, place, or thing that widens the gap between the haves and the have nots. As essential as this timeline is in charting our path forward, it is not the main reason I decided to spend the better part of the past five years on this project. My primary goal which has been growing more and more important as time has gone by: to illuminate the beauty that has sprung into existence from the hands, mind, heart, and soul of my friend and brother Arne Roosman; and, show how despite the ugliness of the hatred he has experienced so intimately since his childhood, choosing love and compassion for others is always in our best interest.

As I sat there arranging and rearranging the piles of paper, I switched on my voice recorder to listen to our conversation and fill in the blanks.

It was early May 1945 when again, the Roosmans were on the move, this time along with 11-million other displaced people in Ally-occupied Germany. Not too long after the Allies arrived in Schwerin, Arne and his family were loaded onto the back of a truck and taken to a Transitional Camp, where they would stay for a couple weeks at a time, until they were transferred to the Oxford DP Camp near Lübeck, Germany. There they would stay for almost the next two years, while the Allies sorted out where everyone was going, and how they were going to get there.

Arne, like most of the world at the time, was familiar with the City of Lübeck before the Roosmans were housed there. The reason for the city's notoriety had nothing to do with its historic old town or its six historic church towers, each reaching skyward more than 100 metres. The reason Lübeck was so well known, Arne said, was because it was the first German city to face heavy bombing by the United Kingdom's Royal Air Force. After the raid the German police reported that 301 people were killed, 783 injured, and more than 15,000 people lost their homes.

"That bombing was sort of a shock to a lot of the world, not the militaristic kind of bums, because it was the first time that the Allies bombed just to make a point," Arne said.

"What point were they trying to make?" I asked.

"They [The British] made a good point, but every time war people make a good point, civilians must suffer. We know that. They picked Lübeck because that was one of the cities in Germany that was totally unattached to the war effort. They could have bombed somewhere down the road, industrial complexes where they could have bombed the shit out of some factories, to weaken Hitler's power. Instead, they wanted to make a point, the Allies– the English in this case– said, 'Look, we don't fuck around. We even kill children.' And they killed a lot of children in Lübeck... Just like the Germans hit London to make sure that the English understood 'We don't fart around. We can kill your Prime Minister right at his desk.' They were sending the same message of war."

"What was Helle doing at that time?" I asked.

"She wasn't in that great shape after having seven kids and not having much to eat. She had the usual wartime fair, a lousy diet. People had hardly anything to eat. Later, when the allies got pissed off with the Estonian un-Germans, we were not welcomed by them. We were in a big compound of the former Reich. All the barracks were taken over by the Allies to accommodate the refugees. And we were part of the refugees. There were nine of us by then, and we lived in one room, twice the size of this kitchen. There were four wooden double beds, and a table in the middle where we ate soup, soup, soup, potato soup, pea soup, beet soup, soup, soup, soup. From all that lousy nourishment I had a boil under my left arm for more than three months. Two weeks of pea soup, two weeks of corn soup. Everything would be corn, corn soup, corn beef, corn bread, corn, corn, corn. Then it would switch to peas; pea soup, pea cake – they were actually pancakes made of peas. You know, you eat what you can."

"My grandmother, who was born the same year as you, hated soup, because I guess that's all she ate during the war."

"In the kitchens there would be huge vats of soup. There'd be people lining up with big containers. You would go down to the soup kitchen, and you would get it filled up and you would take it home. That's how you would eat. With the soup you would get the bread, and the cakes."

"And there were nine of you in such a small room."

"And we lived like that for a couple of years. People don't know how well they have it."

"That's very true. We take a lot for granted these days."

"The Unhappy Mother of a Happy Hunter (Rough Sketch)",
Arne Roosman, pencil on paper, 2021.

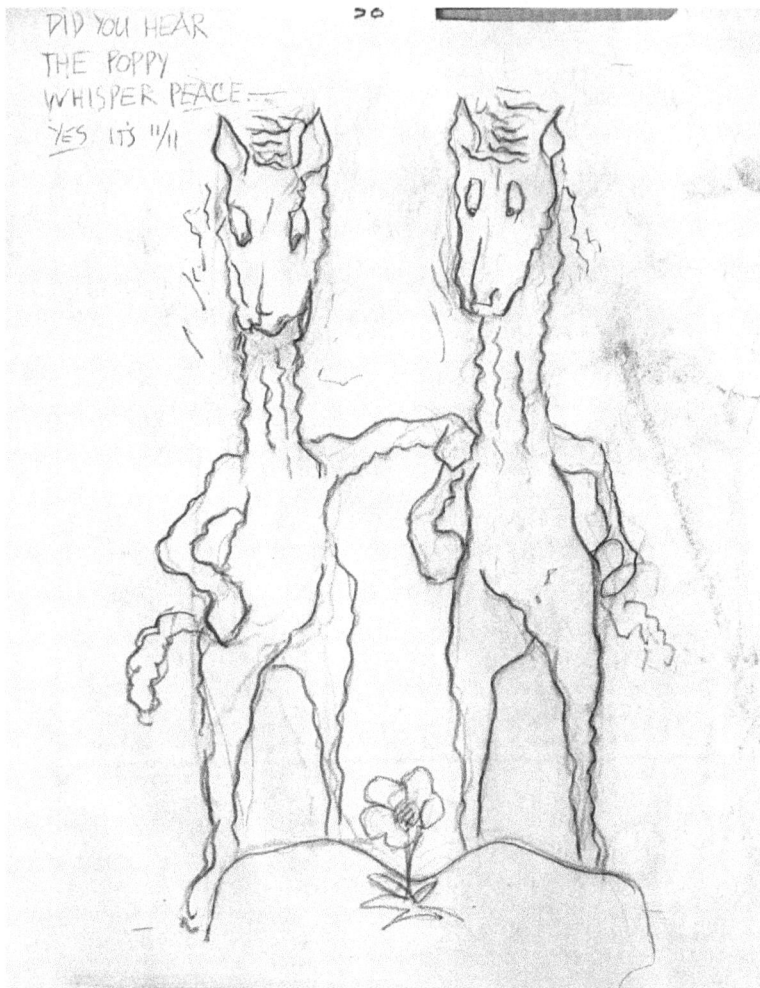

"Did You Hear the Poppy Whisper Peace? Yes it's 11/11",
Arne Roosman, pencil on paper, 2021.

We need the vision of interbeing—we belong to each other;
we cannot cut reality into pieces.
The well-being of 'this' is the well-being of 'that's,
so we have to do things together.
Every side is 'our side'; there is no evil side.
Veterans have experience that makes them the light at the tip of the candle,
illuminating the roots of war, and the way to peace.
–Thich Nhat Hanh, 1991

WAR IS OVER

Although the Nazis had unconditionally surrendered after Hitler offed himself, the war raged on in Japan for the next few months. During that time, the Allies were producing two kinds of atomic bombs: Little Boy, and the Fat Man. On August 6 the U.S.A. dropped a Little Boy on Hiroshima killing anywhere from 90,000 to 146,000 people. Three days later they dropped a Fat Man on Nagasaki killing another 60,000 to 80,000 people. Many more died in the months to follow from radiation sickness, burns, and other injuries that were caused by the bombings. Resources were scarce, and malnutrition was taking its toll on the survivors.

While news of the bombings in Japan and its aftermath were published in the August 7, 1945 edition of *The Toronto Daily Star*, the official end of the Second World War was not reported in *The Bancroft Times* until the August 16, 1945 edition hit the stands. The headline on the top of page one, declared: "HOSTILITIES CEASE WITH JAPAN'S SURRENDER: Nearly Six Years of War Ends With Capitulation of Japan" (*The Bancroft Times* 1945).

Without mentioning a word about the atomic bombs used to obliterate Hiroshima and Nagasaki less than two weeks earlier, *The Bancroft Times* stated the following:

The announcement Tuesday night that Japan had surrendered in accordance with allied surrender terms made at Potsdam, came as a relief of joy, following nearly six years of war, in which many homes of the nation had been bereaved by the loss of sons and fathers who paid the supreme sacrifice that we might enjoy peace once more. To the men who fought and died for the ideals, which we cherish, we owe a debt of gratitude, and thanks, which can never be repaid... following the news of the Jap surrender, church bells rang, automobiles raced through the streets with horns blaring, trucks, loaded with children and grown-ups, joined in hilarious celebration with the news of the end of hostilities.
- *The Bancroft Times,* 1945

"Nagasaki after the bomb" photo series in *The Bancroft Times,* August 16, 1945.

ROAD BACK to new life in Nagasaki. Families, like one above with loaded cart, trek in to find homes.

CLEANUP of ruined city is under way, as picture above shows. Roadway is open for at least one-way traffic and homeless victims of Nagasaki atomic bomb gather possessions and hunt shelter. This photo was taken in center of devastated area.

NEW HOME for bombed-out Nagasaki family above is built from pieces of tin found among debris. Mother and her son are eating their usual meal—rice. Photo is one of first showing rebirth of city.

BOMBED-OUT occupant of home that stood in place of this ~~~es of rubble in Nagasaki has found new place to live. Jap char-acters on the board give his new address.

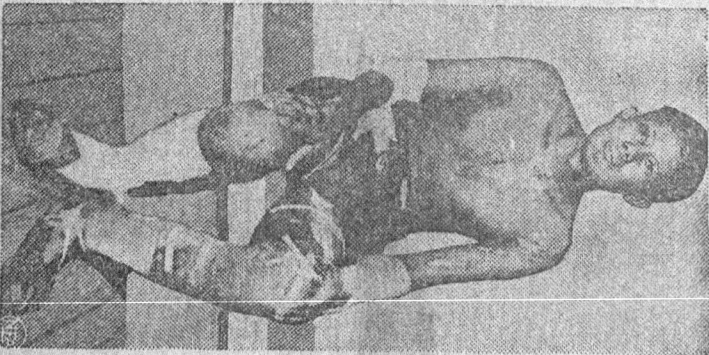

BURNED atomic bomb vic-tim above was Japanese pris-oner of Japs at Nagasaki.

"Nagasaki after the bomb" photo series in *The Bancroft Times*, August 16, 1945.

214

THE LEFT-FOOTED BLUES

While at the Oxford Camp, Arne said his father was democratically elected to take care of matters for the Estonians at the camp. Serving as a shopkeeper of sorts, one of Axel's responsibilities in this role included distributing the shipments of supplies from the United Nations Relief and Rehabilitation Administration (UNRRA) to the refugees at the camp.

There was one shipment from UNRRA that Axel distributed which makes Arne laugh every time he thinks of it. At first glance, Arne said his father told him that the shipment looked normal; just crates full of shoes arriving at camp from the good old U.S.A. Upon closer inspection, however, Arne said his Dad discovered that the footwear was all curiously right-footed.

"Somebody on the other side of the big pond in the U.S.A. had taken a lot of trouble to annoy us, barefoot DPs," he laughed

Arne said there was a woman at camp who had come up with a brilliant idea to trim the leather off the shoes and sew these pieces into beautiful bags made of a patchwork mosaic. All this with Axel's approval, but to the envy of many of the women at camp.

To help dispel the miserable reality of everyday camp life, Axel also got involved with keeping everyone entertained. On one occasion, he wrote a play based on the life of Ulo, a character of Estonian folklore from a novel by Anna Kohver. It was about Ulo's struggle to lead his youthful buddies in taking charge of their community. To prove his and their worth, the gang had to catch and kill a bear.

Axel built the beast and dragged it up on stage for its confrontation with the hunting spheres of the youthful heroes portrayed by his three sons.

Of Axel's three sons, the youngest, Benny, had by now earned the well-deserved stage name, "Oxford Benny", and achieved stardom around camp, Arne said. Two of his sisters, Ingrid and Marit, were engaged by Papa Axel as well. The girls joined the girl guides, and the boys were introduced to Lord Baden Powell's serious study of scouting.

"My sisters were an exception," he said. "They had a father, some noisy brothers, and a mama. Most kids had no Papa ... shot and killed in all that war. Widowed mothers, dating Estonian prisoners of war, released from detention camps, formerly men of ill repute in Belgium. It was a mess and a mix. All that was left over from the war was trees, people, widows, children, veterans, missing limbs, pride, and looks."

"And brains?" I asked with a grin.

"Good question!" he said. "I'm not so sure about the brains."

"Christmas Tree Ablaze", *Cameron Dreamshare,* mixed media on paper, 2025.

Young and old had assembled, waiting for the festivities to begin.
The 30-foot tree had been raised.
Its golden star of Bethlehem, reaching the rafters.
Cellophane streamers, secured from neighbouring wartime munitions works,
imposing, like flaxen hair on a fairytale maiden.
– Arne Roosman

CHRISTMAS EVE 1946

The candles were ready to be lit, as the choir began
singing. Arne said he could pick out the soprano voices of his
favourite classmates. As Axel's assigned helpers lifted their matches
to light the candles on the tree, he said the singing faded into silence;
that silence turned into a whisper, "then words, spoken louder, with
a sense of panic. By now, the decor was like a beautiful couture, all in
flames, then collapsing into a blanket of Black snow. Flakes, slowly
descending from above and covering the well-dressed crowd, many
in white. Dressed in clean, light, sky blue."

Arne remembers watching his festive attire grow darker
and darker as the ashy flurries fell. This was the Roosmans' first
Christmas at Camp Oxford Dragahn near Dannenberg in post-war
West Germany.

"Change is made of choices, and choices are made of character."
— Amanda Gorman, 2021

"BLACK LIVES MATTER", *Arne Roosman*, mixed
media on paper, 2021.

RACISM WITHOUT BORDERS

It was May 25, 2023–exactly three years since former Minneapolis police officer Derek Chauvin murdered George Floyd in broad daylight, in front of a shocked camera-carrying audience of onlookers–when Arne and I found ourselves at a pub in Peterborough talking about the institutional racism he had witnessed within the ranks of the American military after the war. He said the way that the American military treated its own Black troops made him think twice about how the Americans define "Freedom" in the "The Land of the Free, and the home of the Brave."

Acknowledging the ideological divisions in camp, Arne said the usual fights between teenagers almost always took on political colouring; reds versus blues, whites, but no Blacks yet. Arne said it wasn't until the Americans showed up that he saw his first Black person. To his surprise, the U.S. Army did not just keep the white and Black soldiers segregated, he said, "They were actually fenced in."

"In Europe, you didn't have this problem. I saw a Black person for the first time when the Americans liberated Europe. They kept them segregated behind walls... You stood in line for about half an hour just to get a loaf of bread, so every day you would have these conversations with English speaking local Germans. I asked them in German why all the coloured troops were being kept behind this barbed wire, and what they had done to deserve to be behind barbed wire. They told me that was the American culture to keep blacks and whites separate."

"Stop This Menace: Come On Canada! Buy the New Victory Bonds", Ad in *The Bancroft Times*. February 26, 1942.

"You mentioned in, I think it was *A Touch of Arsenic* 1 or 2, how America was losing its mystique and appeal when you learned about the civil rights struggles, and the lynchings in the U.S.A.."

"We had a couple of super headlines out of the U.S.A. that were welcomed by the German press, because the Americans came to tell them how to treat humanity when they were killing Jews. There were a couple of bad cases in the 1940s during the war in the Southern U.S.A. where they hung a group of young Black men for something they didn't do. The German media welcomed this kind of atrocity."

"So that news traveled all the way overseas into a war zone?"

"Well, yeah. If you check history there was something going on in one of the states, where they arrested these Black kids and almost all of them were put to death. I think two survived. It was just one of those famous cases of white guys going after Black kids. They were accused of raping a white woman or something along those lines. The usual story."

"History can be so ugly at times. Too often."

"When these stories got to Europe it made the Yankees look like shit. Once in a while the argument would come up and someone would say, 'You accuse us of killing all these Jews? Look at yourself.' They had a point, but it was a lousy excuse."

THE FREEDOM TO HATE

Recognizing an opportunity to divide and weaken the Allied forces – especially within the American ranks – the Nazis' Ministry of Propaganda attempted to stir up the divisions among white troops and their fellow Black soldiers. Considering the U.S.A. had been legally segregating Black and white Americans since the end of the Civil War through its Jim Crow laws, the American Army's decision to keep its Black troops behind barbed wire fences fit well with the real state of the Union at that time. The end of slavery after the Confederate Army was defeated in the Civil War was still a sore spot for many southern states, who secretly yearned for the "good old days" of the confederacy.

After the First World War and throughout the 1920s, racism was on the rise in the U.S.A. Riding this surging wave of hate, the KKK quickly became one of the biggest organizations in the U.S.A. By 1924, the Klan was reported to have recruited between four and five million members throughout North America. Among their membership in the U.S.A., a couple dozen senators and congressmen were working on the inside to legally keep the nation divided.

In England, racial segregation was not enforced by law as it was in the U.S.A., so many Black American soldiers got a taste of unsegregated freedom during the war.

Back home, many Americans, especially those in the southern states were still living under Jim Crow laws. Therefore, in the "land of the free and the home of the brave", Black and white people were prohibited from getting married. Black Americans were often legally denied treatment by white nurses and doctors. Schools were segregated along racial lines, with Black students being given outdated textbooks, and secondhand football uniforms discarded by white schools. The laws also encouraged businesses to economically exclude the Black community by allowing white business owners to post signs such as "WHITES ONLY", or "COLORED ENTRANCE."

Upon returning home, Black soldiers in the U.S.A. and Canada discovered that the legalized systemic racism they had left behind when they crossed the Atlantic to fight for a free and democratic world, was still thriving and becoming even more insidious.

"Another Slap in the Face", *Arne Roosman,* mixed media on paper, 2021.

ANOTHER SUNNY DAY

It was almost 8 a.m. by the time I made it to Arne's front door on the morning of August 18, 2023. Arne had an appointment with one of the specialists at the hospital in Cobourg, so we made plans to turn the day into a bit of a road trip. On the way there, while sucking in carcinogens from the wildfires burning in a galaxy not at all far, far away, tasting the climate crisis on our breath, Arne told me more about what life was like in the DP camps in post-war Germany.

"We ride!" I said, starting the engine. "Did you have breakfast yet, Arne?"

"I had a little bread with my coffee but not really."

"Me neither. We can grab something on the way then. Tim Hortons maybe?"

"Sounds good."

Getting our bearings with the GPS, we drove for about 10 minutes until we hit the first turn. With the voice coming from the navigation softwareconfirming we were on the right track; we dove into what was on our minds.

"I have been thinking a lot about your time in the DP camps. I have so many questions. My mind is still processing what it must have been like for you and your family, always being on the run from war at such a young age."

"You know, in a way, as a child on the run, you were not on

the run. Kids are kids. It was just another exciting kind of situation: 'Oh, are we now going on board a ship all the way to where?' Then the grown-ups would say, 'Well, we're going to Germany.' We'd say, 'Where's that?' So, then they would say, 'Well, Deutschland.' So they'd show us on a map where Germany is. But as far an eight-year-old goes, it makes no bloody difference where you are. You are not running away from anything; you are just there. Things happen around you and most of the time it is exciting. Once in camp, you're settling down, eating pea soup and potato soup and all that soupy stuff. In the meantime, your kid brother, who is 10-years-old, becomes the Tsar of the black market in this camp with 800 Estonians. He found those wires that go into the electric cooking devices, the spirals. He found about 50-100 of those in some bunker. So he started peddling those, and he made a kid's fortune. See, on the market you can't buy cigarettes, you can't buy matches. Everything is on the black market. So you go into your kitchen, and you plug in your spiral. You can't light your cigarette if you don't have matches. So you go into your kitchen, and you plug in your spiral heater into your electric cooker. Your mother is the smoker, and you don't smoke yet; you have to go and get the cigarette from mother because the kitchen is too far away. So mother gives you the cigarette, because she gets five cigarettes a week from the Allies. A few people start screwing up with the Allies, they start hating all the DPs, because the DPs are ungrateful. Instead of being happy with the cigarettes and the loaf of bread. No, they want the German dark rye. They don't want the white bread of the Allies. So, the Allies get pissed off, and they cut the whole camp off English rations. These are everyday things that were a constant in a situation where people have nothing but what they have on, hardly any underwear. They don't have any private things, except a book, family literature, etc., etc."

"Such a fragile situation," I said. "Was there still a lot of political tension?"

"There were no politics, because the politics were now exhausted. Now the Nazis were dead, the Communists were dead. The Estonians had no pants to put on, because the Russians kept their trousers. So, you were walking around with your bare ass showing. You had nothing. You had no money, you had no cigarettes, you had no food. Really, you were basically just existing. You were at the mercy of some people, like the Allies, UNRRA, the United Nations giving you a little bit to eat here and there. So that you get only so many boils. At least we only have so many armpits."

When it came to what was on the menu at the camp kitchen, Arne said, "Tim Hortons would have been like the Royal York. Breakfast. We were introduced to corned beef. I never tasted anything so good. Fried, a quarter inch thick, with toast on the side. Tea with powdered milk, sugar sweet. Some days pancakes."

Now parked outside the Tim Hortons, before I went inside to pick up our breakfast, I opened my notebook and handed it to Arne. At our last meeting a couple of weeks earlier, Arne had given me a bunch of "snippets", notes, and poetry that he had written in response to a page full of questions I had left for him to have a look at. Most of what he had written helped clarify my confusions, however, as usual there were two sentences that my mind and heart would not allow me to accept. The haunting scrawl of words at the bottom of his answer sheet read: "Russians being deported back to the Soviet Union; a young mother throws her newborn into open pit fire to save it from deportation to Workers' Paradise. This, a sunny afternoon."

"Arne, I have to ask, can you tell me more about what you have written here?" I passed him the note he had written, pointing at the statement that had caused my disbelief.

"That was terrible. They were on transport; the Soviets have been taking British DPs back to Russia. A British politician, Harold Macmillan was in charge of deporting Russian refugees back to the Soviets. He was in cahoots with Stalin, Macmillan, so we hated him. He arranged all these transports to take the Soviet people back to Stalin.... Some of them didn't want to move because they didn't want to go to the Siberian bloody camps, etc. And this mother, she just had a baby – at that time we were traveling right through Lübeck, Durchgangslager – and this mother had just had this baby. In this camp it had big fire pits, open fire pits during the day where they were burning garbage. It was a German army camp originally before it was a camp for DPs. This young mother did not want her child to become one of the workers in Stalin's Siberian Paradise, so she took her newborn and threw it into this open fire pit."

"While it was still alive? Really? Jesus Christ!"

"This is where we grew up. That's when I was 15 years old. That's what you saw, what you heard. That was your situation."

"Where were you when this happened?"

"I was probably around the corner. All I know is that there was this noise, this scream. We were all watching these people going to Siberia. Seeing who they are. And there's truckloads full, Russian trucks. The Russians came into Lübeck to pick up Russian citizens that did not want to go home to the Workers' Paradise. They wanted to stay in these God damn camps and see what they could make out of their new life, post-war. See, they were brought into Germany by the Nazis to serve the Reich as labourers, slave labour. So, Hitler's slave labour was made up of millions of Russians brought from Russia into Germany to make them work, work, work, so that the German boys could go to war, war, war. So now that the country is empty of labour, they bring in the slaves, straight slave labour. They were the Russians, and they had to wear this big Soviet Union sign on them."

"The hammer and sickle?"

"No, no, no ... no nice décor. It was a big 'O' on a blue background. The Jews had the Star, and the Poles had a 'P', and the Estonians didn't have anything. But the Estonian boys that went into the Estonian part of the German army, they had Estonia on their uniform. They were all sort of subdivided into slave labour. This poor woman did not want her child to grow up in a labour camp in Siberia or wherever in Russia, so she threw her newborn into that pit. Those fire pits were half the size of this place, and they were constantly kept on fire, because they were burning documents or whatever was burnable. What the allies did not need, they burned. The war was over. This was 1945. Molotov was telling Macmillan, 'Look, these are my people, these are Russians, my name is Molotov, I'm number two in Russia, and these are my people. So, I want my people home. You bring my people home because Hitler took my people away, made them into slave labour. Now I want them to have the freedom of the proletariat. We are the happiest people in the world.' Macmillan said, 'Done! There you go!' Then he became prime minister a few years later for England. A lot of Russian people never forgave him. Arne Roosman, who isn't even a Russian, never forgave Mr. Macmillan for [his role in] throwing babies into the coals of a burning fire. And I am telling you, I can't...."

Overwhelmed with sadness and rage, Arne's words turned to tears. Taking a deep breath and a sip from his mug of beer, he continued:

"That's the 'freedom-loving' Brits ... the same Brits that went to India 100 years earlier and killed women and children by the hundreds. Lord Kitchener mowed them down in Delhi. Yeah, well, I'm sure you have read your history."

"The same forces that set up the residential school system in Canada which killed so many Indigenous children."

"There you go," affirmed Arne. "We are all Angels, because Angels are the meanest thing that the Catholic religion ever invented. We are all Angels, and I'm an Angel too. And you are all ancient. But there are different Angels. There are the Angels that get thrown into fire pits after they become babies, and I'm one of them that just didn't make it into the fire pit. Yeah, but I understood I should have been in the fire pit, because I was one of the Angels that did not want to be liberated by these fucking forces."

"Sounds as wonderful as the Americans' liberation of Iraq. Never mind the millions of people that died, or the depleted uranium left behind to poison children."

"You know, humanity is such a shitty outfit sometimes."

"Unfortunately, I agree, Arne."

"I don't like to go back there because I get carried away. I become one of those bad Angels because I almost can feel hatred inside me. And I don't like that. I don't like to feel that hatred, but it wants to come. That bad Angel in you wants to take over, you know. What makes the Angel the Devil is that very sensation, 'Oh yeah, I'll get you!'

"Revenge! Vengeance," I said.

"That's what they say. They say, 'Oh yeah, if you're going to burn babies, then I'm going to burn babies and the mother of the babies too!'" Arne said as he adjusted his glasses to wipe away the tears which had again started to run down his cheeks.

"Then the escalation begins," I said.

"You know, Nate, in a way, sometimes I don't want to go back there. But then again, at the same time, it is a story that has to be told. Silence was never, never, never a good way to go. So whenever I get sort of a little bit carried away I remind myself that silence never helped anybody."

"What did Gandhi say, something about 'An eye for an eye making the whole world blind.' Then again if someone kills or harms someone you love, it's natural to want to even the score."

"It seems the only way to get justice is through injustice," Arne said.

"It's a never-ending cycle where everybody ends up hating each other."

"That incident with the baby is very much in my memory. I don't think I saw her doing it. I don't think so, but I didn't have to. We were playing on the third floor of the barracks. We knew how to get into the third floor, and it was empty for some reason. It was some sort of storage. So, we were roaming around there when somebody said, 'The Russians are taking people again!' So, we ran out from the third floor – there were these big brick buildings, concrete three-storey buildings all over the place – and the Russians were coming through picking up people. Of course, the Town of Lübeck is all around. So we all ran out, and that's when I could ... I can hear the baby ... sometimes it's like a dreamscape, because everybody was screaming, 'They threw a baby in the fire! They threw a baby in the fire! Before you know it you can actually hear the baby screaming, dying in the fire, 'Ahhhhhh!' Even for those who didn't hear it, in your head you still can because everyone is yelling, 'There's a baby in the fire!' And there was nothing you could do about it. There you are, a 15-year-old, and there is a baby in the fire."

The horror of that day, while carved deeply into his consciousness, lingers in his memory as a recurring nightmare. In its wake, Arne said he often found himself questioning whether he was actually there and heard the baby screaming. What he does remember about that day, however, is that "'twas a sunny day." He also remembers clearly hearing the voices of people in camp shouting, 'They threw a baby in the fire!'– words he has been unable to forget.

"A simple statement implying that more babies will be ending up in other fires, because if one mother could do it, why not another mother?"

"Just awful, Arne. That changes everything from that point on. I am sorry that you had to experience that."

"You know, the funny thing is that all these horrible, horrible things, happened on sunny days," Arne said. "And in Germany, the sun does not shine every day. It's mostly rain... It was just my urging," he added. "I had to have it on a sunny day. On the worst days the sun had to shine, or else I wouldn't have been able to live through it."

"Either you lose hope completely and you shatter and break into pieces, or you become so resilient that no one can break you anymore."
— Malala Yousafzai, 2019

THE TRAIN THROUGH HAMBURG

It was January 1948 when the Roosmans left the discomforts of the Oxford DP Camp in Lübeck to try for "Sunny" Sweden. Although the war had been over for more than two years, much of Germany, and all of Europe for that matter, lay in ruin. With more than 40-million Displaced Persons looking for a place to call home, tensions were often high amongst those on the move. The world had changed, and was still transforming as a new world order was taking shape.

In the spring of 2024, April 11th, Arne recounted his family's slow journey by train, through the war-ravaged German City of Hamburg.

As we sat there in his backyard, sipping red wine and catching a few rays, Arne told me of his arduous trek to freedom. His description of the post-apocalyptic landscape, polluted by war and ruin, is a testament to the fact that again humanity is choosing to repeat the same self-destructive patterns we always seem to revisit, this time in Palestine and Ukraine. Two days before our visit, several major news networks around the world reported that the Israeli government had killed at least 14 people in an attack on al-Zawaida in central Gaza's Nuseirat refugee camp. In another Israeli air strike on a Palestinian Refugee Camp, *Aljazeera* announced that three sons and four grandchildren of Hamas leader Ismail Haniyeh were killed in an Israeli air attack on a Gaza refugee camp. Less than two weeks earlier, on April 22 – Earth Day – the United Nations, confirmed that among the 34,151 Palestinians killed, up to that point, some

14,685 were children and 9,670 women. The UN also acknowledged that there were at least another 7,000 corpses rotting beneath the rubble.

On February 24, 2024 – the two-year anniversary of Russia's invasion of Ukraine – the United Nations Human Rights Office of the High Commissioner released a report providing an update on the war (OUNHCHR 2024). In this report, the UN stated that overall civilian casualties since Russia invaded Ukraine on February 24, 2022, at least 10,582 civilians had been killed, while another 19,875 were injured. Reading through the reports and scanning the images of intense but avoidable suffering we can't seem to stop causing, I recalled the words that flowed from the spirit of Gonzo journalist Hunter S. Thompson, through his typewriter and onto the page after the attacks on the World Trade Centre in Manhattan on September 11th, 2001. While events were still unfolding and the world was trying to make sense of the violence, he wrote: "The towers are gone now, reduced to bloody rubble, along with all hopes for Peace in Our Time, in the United States or any other country. Make no mistake about it: We are At War now -- with somebody -- and we will stay At War with that mysterious Enemy for the rest of our lives. ...It will be a Religious War, a sort of Christian Jihad, fueled by religious hatred and led by merciless fanatics on both sides. It will be guerilla warfare on a global scale, with no front lines and no identifiable enemy" (Thompson 2001).

Then, as they do now, his words beg the question: why choose war when peace is always a better option?

If my exchanges with Arne have taught me anything, it is that through the fire, the smoke, and the dust stirred up by our slaughter, the sun keeps shining. He has also shown me how in war there is no justice for the 'winners' or 'losers', because in the end, all war offers are fear and pain. Instead of leaving behind a legacy of peace, we are inevitably left: counting the lives needlessly taken, helping those crippled by trauma to heal, and, waiting for those corrupted by an insatiable lust for revenge to unleash their fury.

From April 18 until May 3, 1945, the City of Hamburg was the stage for what would become one of the final battles of the Second World War. Before a single shot was fired in the final offensive on Nazi forces in Hamburg by the British, most of the city had already been destroyed during Operation Gomorrah at the end of July 1943. Over the course of four nights – July 24, 27, 29 and August 2 – Brittain's RAF attacked Hamburg with an unprecedented 3,000 bombers.

As a result of the Nazis' blitz on London, the Brits knew that igniting the incendiaries being stored there would do far greater damage than bombs alone. Hamburg contained a significant number of 'military targets', and in the unseasonably dry conditions leading up to the raids, the RAF strategically bombed the city with the intention of destroying it. The bombing stewed up a deadly and monstrous fire tornado that reached skyward some 460 metres (1510 feet) high. According to a study on the aerial bombings by researchers from Stanford's Department of Computer Science, one survivor of the raids described the carnage as follows:

> With hurricane force, 150 mile per-hour winds were sucked into the oxygen vacuum created by the fire, ripping trees out by their roots, collapsing buildings, pulling children out of their mothers' arms. Twenty square miles of the city centre burned in an inferno that would rage for nine full days. ... The temperature in the firestorm reached 1,400 degrees Fahrenheit. There was no oxygen to breathe; whatever was flammable burst spontaneously into flame.
> - **Raid survivor, Stanford 2004**

Although 100+ kilometres away from Hamburg that day in Schwerin, Arne recalled his memory of that horrendous day.

"You could see a red light glowing on the horizon and in the sky over Hamburg," he said.

"Were you not in Schwerin?"

"Oh yeah," he said. "We were more than 100 kilometres away, but you could still see this ominous red glow. We could hear it too. There was this constant groaning, like thunder rumbling in the distance."

In the attack, more than half the city was levelled, more than 1 million people were rendered homeless, and an estimated 37,000 to 46,000 civilians lost their lives. More collateral damage demanding a response from the survivors.

After the British had captured Hamburg in early May 1945 – the Nazis' last remaining pocket of resistance in the north – the majority of the surviving Nazi troops retreated into the Jutland Peninsula in northern Germany. The British 7th Armoured Division then continued onward to Lübeck where the Roosman family was anticipating the arrival of their "liberators."

"Have you seen the pictures that are coming out of Gaza right now?" Arne asked, handing me an article he had clipped from a newspaper that featured recent photographs of the devastation in Palestine. "It's all ruins. It's totally flattened to the earth."

"I know! Just piles of rubble, flesh, blood, and bone," I said, taking a big chug of beer to wash down the news. "You told me before about how after the war people in Germany were just existing; just existing, that's how I would describe the people in the pictures coming out of Palestine right now. They remind me of how you described your trip through Hamburg after the war."

"That's what it looked like," he said. "There were just chimneys standing up everywhere. The train barely moved 20 miles an hour. It was a landscape of ruins. All chimneys, chimneys, chimneys, thousands of chimneys."

"What was the atmosphere like on the train? I can imagine it must have been a pretty chaotic scene."

"The people riding the train were all over the train. They were sitting on top of the train, they were sitting on the stairs of the train, because the train was always too full. I was sitting in the window, Dad handed stuff through the window to me and as I pulled it into the train, this German next to me said, 'Keep that shit luggage out of my seat.' My dad said back to him, 'This luggage is going to Sweden.' That shut the Kraut up. Now he knew we were going to a neutral country, he was jealous. He was sitting there giving us dirty looks. That's how Axel and Helle had to travel with us seven kids; travelling on a train where everyone hates you because they are jealous you are going to Sweden."

"Where were your grandparents during the war?"

"Grandmother and grandfather stayed in the Russian zone in eastern Germany. It took them a couple of years to get out of East Germany and join us in West Germany. Several years later, grandpa was already dead, but grandmother came to Sweden. It was a couple of years after the war was over and almost forgotten. It's amazing how quickly things are forgotten."

*"Miles upon miles of the ruins of the great Port of Hamburg,
illustrating the annals of war.
Slowly, slowly, our train would move, carrying us northward.
Flensburg, then Halseingborg, then the ferry over the waves to sweet Sweden.
Peaceful and rich Sweden.
With some Swedish ancestry in the Roosman-Boesberg Clan,
we were welcomed to this northern paradise."*
– Arne Roosman

"Burning Forest/Ashes on the Highway in Northern Ontario", *Arne Roosman,* watercolour on paper, 1976.

The "Law of Love" is as fundamental,
and as universal as any other physical law.
It is written everywhere we look,
and it maps our intimate connection
with the rest of the living world.
– Dr. David Suzuki, 1997

THERE'S FIRE IN THE FOREST

I am walking slowly through the forest, feeling its breath struggle. It is June 13, 2023 in Ontario and the trees are again trading oxygen, shelter, soil, pollen, and water for respect. But respect, as we all know, is both mutual and earned. To the north, east, and west critical habitat is being incinerated, life is being destroyed and communities of animals, including humans, are on the run for their lives. We are waging war against our home planet and ourselves.

Humanity, as Arne might say, has against our own best interests, become the "Official Opposition" within Earth's political system.

Certainly, with their underground social network of intertwining roots, the trees surrounding and towering over me here in L'Amable, roughly 150 kilometres away from the closest flames, know deep down what is going on and who is responsible. Yet still, despite the awareness they store in their rings and limbs, they continue to bestow upon us the clean air, clean water, healthy soil, and healthy habitat that we need to live.

That morning before I went for a hike, then Emergency Preparedness Minister Bill Blair announced that 47,000 square kilometres of forests had already been swallowed up by the fires, and that 431 wildfires were still burning across the country. In Edson, Alberta, 8,400 residents were placed under an evacuation order, while hundreds of people in B.C. had already fled their homes or were in limbo on the edge of evacuation. A testament to the catastrophic magnitude of the worsening crisis, some 5,000 firefighters from several countries joined the nationwide fight against the wildfires in Canada.

The air smelled of a campfire, every breath leaving behind an aftertaste like that of a charred hot dog. Finding a perfectly placed fallen tree to set up my backcountry office for the afternoon, I took out my notebook, recorder, and thermos full of coffee, and made myself comfortable.

Before switching on the recorder to listen to our conversation, I took a moment to appreciate my coffee and the peace of the forest. In the poplar tree behind me there was a robin singing. In front of me a pair of black and white warblers darted in and out of the low-hanging limbs of a spruce grove.

If it wasn't for the toxic smoke burning my eyes and lungs, the terrible fiery reality that was unfurling in a rash of wildfires that stretched across the country, would—like the climate crisis before the 2023 wildfire season—be out of sight and out of mind: exactly where the fossil fuel industry wished it would stay. But, as our rapidly heating planet keeps showing us, nature doesn't respond very well to wishes. Rather than wishing for the climate crisis to go away on its own, while continuing to kill the planet for short-term profits, Big Oil would be wise to heed the advice that the fictional character Willie T. Soke offered his pal Thurman Merman in the 2003 film, Bad Santa: "Wish in one hand, shit in the other one; see which one fills up first."

During our symposium on June 7, 2023 Arne shared with me his thoughts on the recent appearance of 'Local Smoke', Nature, God, and the essence of existence. Leaning back against the trunk of the fallen tree, I hit play on my recorder to listen to our conversation from the first day that the smoke appeared over North Hastings.

"What do you think of all these wildfires? Have you ever experienced smoke like this before?" I asked Arne.

"No, never. This is new to me."

"I stepped outside this morning and couldn't tell what the hell was going on. I thought one of my neighbours' houses might be on fire or something."

"They were talking about it on the radio this morning and *CBC* is saying this bloody smoke is only going to get worse."

"I heard that on my way here as well."

"I don't know, Nate. What are we going to do?"

"I don't know either, Arne. For decades the scientific community has been telling us we were going to hit a tipping point with the climate sometime soon. Hopefully this wasn't it. At least now those who were saying climate change is a hoax can't deny it anymore."

"Oh, yes they can!" Arne chirped back. "Come on, Nate, you know the facts don't matter these days."

"Yeah, that's true," I said disappointedly, knowing he was right. "They do love their 'alternative facts'. That was one of the things I talked about with Bob Woodward after the taping of that TVO Today special in Toronto last winter."

"Which one was he again?" Arne asked.

"He's one half of the journalist team that helped take down Richard Nixon. I interviewed him the day after my friend and I almost got stuck here in that big snowstorm."

"Ah, that's right, it was him and Carl Bernstein. What did you ask him?"

"I asked him how as journalists are we supposed to cover the news when there is a growing number of loudmouths on the far-right, who are happy to embrace 'alternative facts' over scientifically proven and supported facts."

"What did he say?" inquired Arne.

"Basically, he said it is up to us as journalists to set a high bar for ourselves in terms of accuracy. He also said that we need to be patient and diligent with fact checking. He told me about how he had received a whole bunch of memos from Trump's former lawyer Rudy Giuliani to Republican Senator Lindsey Graham, which claimed more than 250,000 prisoners in Wisconsin voted on election day in 2020. Apparently after they investigated his claims, they weren't able to find a single one. The fact that they were able to investigate these allegations and reveal how they were 100 per cent false proves that the truth still matters."

"Your lie can become my truth, because if I repeat your lie then some people will say well, Arne said so."

"That's the dangerous thing with the internet, too many people think just because they saw something on the internet, it's got to be true."

"That's right. My grandmother more than 80 years ago told me, because her husband was a printer and he printed a newspaper for a while at his home, and to her the printed word was God's gospel. The Bible is printed, and if you print something that is forever, and it comes from forever, so it is the truth. 'Nobody would spend ink on a lie, would they? People are not that stupid. Come on Arne, wake up!' That's what she thought."

"It makes sense though," I responded.

According to Arne, his Grandmother would tell him, 'The smart people print, and they print the truth, because they know the truth. You and I, we don't know the truth Arne, but the printer, he knows the truth because he, your grandpa the printer, would not waste one bloody kopeck on a lie.'"

"Now, with social media it's so easy to spread bull shit. I stay away from it as much as possible but then get sucked in whenever I learn of something insane going on in the news."

"There are a lot of grandmas who are not grandmas yet, but they will be one day just like my grandma, only it will not be the printed word, it will be the word on the bloody screen," said Arne. "So, they'll say, 'Nobody would waste a machine like this for $300 and have lies on it? Come on.'"

"This is where I think Trump changed the game," I said. "Even though it was kind of heading in that direction, Trump took it over the hill. With all his lies he normalized lying. They even came up with the term 'alternative facts.' What the fuck is an alternative fact anyway? As far as I'm concerned, the only alternative to a fact is bull shit."

"The facts are the facts," Arne said, "so they'll always be there waiting for the bull shitters."

"Speaking of bull shit, have you heard of this new Republican Congressman George Santos, Arne? He pretty much lied about everything to get elected... and then he got in."[21]

"Well yeah, but when you listen to him, you know he really knows what we should be doing," Arne said in the voice of a Santos voter.

"If what we know is true is allowed to be interpreted as false, there's really no ground to stand on. Shit! Maybe the Earth is flat."

"That's one of the problems," he said. "Debate has been curtailed because now gossip has become debate."

"I think the media is partly to blame. Look at climate change for instance; when they first started to report on it, they would give as much airtime, if not more, to the people being paid by the oil companies to deny its existence as they would give to scientists who dedicated their lives to understanding the Earth's climate. So basically, the words of a handful of spokespeople who are paid by the fossil fuel industry are given as much weight as tens of thousands of scientists from around the world."

"What is going to become of us Nate? We all have to go back to school; but who is going to decide what we learn?"

"That reminds me of Florida's Governor Ron DeSantis. Trump was a huge supporter of him, he was a huge supporter of

---

21   A report in The Guardian entitled, "George Santos's weirdest lies revisited as he pleads guilty to fraud" listed the many lies of former New York congressman George Santos. According to *The Guardian*, Santos lied about: having been a Brazilian drag performer; producing the Broadway musical Spider-Man: Turn Off the Dark; having been a star volleyball player at a New York college he never attended; being a Wall Street big shot; having Jewish heritage; running a pet charity called Friends of Pets United. He did not. But he raised $3,000 for a surgery on a service dog belonging to a disabled Navy veteran. However, the dog wasn't sick. Santos took the money anyway (Helmore 2024).

Trump, but when he was running in the primaries, Trump started talking shit about him. Oh yeah, and his wife, as usual. Anyways, 'Meatball Ron', as Trump called him, passed a law preventing teachers from teaching about slavery, racism, homosexuality; they can't even say 'gay' in the classroom apparently anymore. How queer is that?"

"Next they start burning the books," Arne said, shaking his head.

"Well, they've already banned a ton of books. There are all these images going around online of libraries and schools with empty bookshelves. Yet somehow this clown still positions himself as an advocate for 'free' speech. Kids in Florida won't even have the opportunity to learn about slavery at school. It will be as if it never happened."

"Why don't you teach my kids something good!" Arne said in the voice of an angry parent.

"Well Mr. Roosman, teaching about slavery makes white kids feel bad," I barked back as the Teacher.

"Just because Black children felt bad for around 400 years or more, that doesn't mean that you need to teach things that make white kids feel bad," I continued as the parent.

"What about the truth? What about history? Don't we need to teach history, Mr. Roosman?" the Teacher asked.

"The truth is something that conveniently can be used by any liar," he said. "There is no truth that a good liar will not use. You can really bend these things; these philosophical ideas."

"I think Mother Nature is starting to dish out some hard truths with the climate now. There's not a lot of time to spew bull shit when you're trying to keep your head above water or run away from a fire."

"Well Nate, that's what life is all about, surviving. No, we can't run away from the creator. Not in the religious sense. Science."

"Who is this guy that is always saying he's going to Mars? I keep on forgetting his name."

"Musk, Elon Musk. He's something else!"

"Oh yeah, totally nuts!" Arne stated with conviction. "But what can we do, he owns the world. He has more bloody money than some entire countries."

"It's obscene," I said.

"It's unbelievable how this capitalist system allows that kind of idiotic wealth," Arne said. "Nobody needs that kind of money to do whatever they want to do, or to sustain their lifestyle. It's unbelievable."

"I know! Why the hell are we talking about minimum wage when there are individuals with more wealth than entire nations? I don't get it either, Arne. Around the same time Musk was bragging that he was going to Mars, and he was planning to buy Twitter for $44 billion, I saw a report in the news from the United Nations indicating that it would cost around $1 billion to end the famine in East Africa. So there are about 7.1 million people throughout Somalia and East Africa who are literally starving, because of a famine caused by a drought, which is the result of a climate crisis that we in the west are predominantly responsible for. There are more than 2,700 billionaires in the world and none of them – or even better yet, all of them combined – can't come up with $1 billion to potentially save millions of lives? We need to get our priorities straight."

"Well, he is a 'businessman', you know. He likes Trump, because Trump is a 'businessman' too. There is no reason that kind of wealth should be permitted. And it's not even illegal what he's doing."

"I know, eh. That's the scary part," I said.

Cats didn't start as mousers. Weasels and snakes and dogs are more efficient as rodent-control agents.
I postulate that cats started as psychic companions, as Familiars, and have never deviated from this function.
- William S. Burroughs, 1986

"Arne and Latte", photograph by *N. Smelle, 2025.*

BASTET'S DIVINITY

"What do you think, Latte?" Arne asked, stroking him behind the ears gently. "T.S. Elliot wrote about cats; I think I have his cat book. To him, cats were the supreme being. It's great when they respond in a human fashion, and you recognize that they also have brains. People look down on animals as stupid, but it's amazing how well functioning their brains are."

"I get it. My cat Onyx and I lived alone here for a few years, and he communicates better than most humans I know. His awareness of what's going on around him is at another level. The ancient Egyptians and some Buddhists believe that cats share a connection with the Divine as well. Wiccans too."

"They are very in tune when you pay attention to them," he said. "Strange how all the religions seem to intermingle here and there. They didn't know which way to go, and we are so helpless in our quest to try and figure out the Universe that we need somebody else. We can't just trust that we are these phenomena, and that there might be other phenomena like us from other planets. We always need some sort of top guy, a leader. We can't seem to get by without a king, or a queen, or a God."

"We always need a villain too," I said.

"Oh yeah, sure, because 'I' would never do anything bad," said Arne. "It's the 'Devil' in me. We need the bad guys to give us a reason to be good."

"So, it's out of boredom, that God created the Devil?" I asked Arne.

"This is what makes God so human. This is what we don't

want to acknowledge; that this 'God' is 'me' and 'you' and everyone. 'God' and 'I' are the same thing."

"And we are part of Nature, or 'God', no matter what we choose to call that energy – Jehovah, Allah, Buddha, etc. – it is present in all living things."

"It is strange how God makes it into every book," said Arne. "My question is: Why God? And which God? Reading all these beautiful ideas on the wonders of science that we spend zillions of dollars trying to figure out, we keep on coming to that conclusion. Why can't we accept that strange sentiment, that because 'it' is, 'it' is. It's not that somebody makes 'it', say a creative God. This is what the human brain cannot absorb; the very fact that 'it' is, is only because 'it' is. Why would there be a purpose to kill 10 million mosquitoes every day? They have thinking mechanisms. See, we are so proud of our fucking brain, well, actually our brain isn't that good. You go into the depths of the ocean, and there is that huge monster; its eyes are 11 and a half inches across. And these two huge eyes of the sea monster see more than we can even think and dream up. This monster that cannot put it on paper and write a Bible. But if you go into Biblical kind of prospects of all these bums from three thousand years ago, they look stupid compared to this sea monster... So, what I accept is the fact that the whole Universe, and all the existence of these phenomenal things, everything has the resilience of brains in it. There are little creeps here between the cracks, tiny little things which also have brain power. It is amazing what these little guys do, only they don't serve our purpose. They're just there; they're almost dust, thinking dust."

"The Universe, Nature are incredible," I said. "The deeper we look into it, the clearer we understand the fact that every living thing has consciousness. Even if you take the time to get to know a tree – not just in terms of identifying one species from the next, but as an individual living organism with its own life story and ecological function – one cannot help but establish a sort of kinship with it. I have always felt a sense of connectedness whenever I spend time in a forest. Still, I was blown away when I learned how trees communicate with each other by using their roots as a kind of subterranean communication system. It's incredible! They share information and resources, and their roots will intertwine and merge with one another to gain stability."

 MacLean's magazine reserved a few pages to consider the "Future of Our Planet" in its April 2024 edition. One of the articles featured Canada's Minister of Natural Resources, the Honourable Jonathan Wilkinson's vision and goals for the rest of the year ahead. "This year," he said, "my goal is to fight climate change while making life more affordable for Canadians." To accomplish his goals, Wilkinson said he has made it one of his top priorities to prepare for the upcoming wildfire, flood, and hurricane seasons. Heading into the first Canadian wildfire season since the worst in recorded history, it makes sense why the Minister is preemptively focused on the fires yet to ignite. In 2023, the cost of fighting the 6,132 wildfires that raged that year exceeded $1 billion. That is a 60 per cent increase compared to the annual average. As long as we continue to inadequately address the causes and consequences of carelessly heating our planet, the cost of our blissful ignorance will continue to rise.

"Eve Under the Apple Tree", *Arne Roosman*, charcoal and conte on paper, 2012.

ALOHA REALITY

Canada was not the only country to be devastated by wildfires in 2023. There was an article by Carolyn Kormann in Arne's November 6, 2023 edition of *The New Yorker,* entitled, "Through the Smoke" that gave a human face to the deadly wildfires that ravaged the Hawaiian island of Maui four months earlier on August 8.

What opened my eyes and dropped my jaw while reading the article was the firsthand account of Lahaina resident Shaun Saribay's bike ride through the aftermath of the fires. Following Saribay on his ride through the smouldering corpse-littered streets on the morning after he had spent the previous night trying to prevent his home – a home that had been his family's for several generations – from being destroyed, Kormann wrote "Saribay recorded videos throughout the night as he fought the fire. Despite his efforts, flames consumed the church. Well after midnight, the men tried to save a neighbouring preschool, but that caught fire, too. When the sun rose and the wind began to ebb, Saribay got on an old bike and rode around town looking for other survivors. 'I'm seeing bodies every fucking way,' he recalled. I'm pedaling through charcoal bodies and bodies that didn't have one speck of burn–they just died of inhalation of black smoke. I felt like I was the only fucking human on Earth" (Kormann 2023).

In the town of nearly 13,000 residents, Kormann reported that 7,200 people were displaced by the fires, and that 22,000 buildings were damaged or destroyed. The cost of the rebuilding was estimated at $5.5 billion. The greatest cost of the fires, however, was measured in human lives. While initially reports announced that the death

"The World is Listening", *Arne Roosman*, mixed media on paper, 2021.

We are about to sacrifice our civilization,
for the opportunity of a very small number of people
to continue to make enormous amounts of money.
We are about to sacrifice the biosphere
so that rich people in countries like mine can live in luxury.
But it is the sufferings of the many which pay for the luxuries of the few.
— Greta Thunberg, 2019

toll had reached 115, the number of dead dropped to 97, when it was discovered that some of the remains had melted together and become "fragmented or commingled."

Early in 2024, NASA confirmed what climatologists all over the world suspected: Earth's average surface temperature in 2023 was the warmest on record.

According to NASA's analysis of climate data collected throughout the previous year, global temperatures were around 2.1 degrees Fahrenheit (1.2 degrees Celsius) above the average for NASA's baseline period (1951-1980), (Bardan 2024).By the time this book was sent to press in the spring of 2025, Roxana Bardan had already written another report indicating that global temperatures are still rising, and that 2024 was now the hottest year on record.[22]

In the announcement on January 12, NASA Administrator Bill Nelson acknowledged that "NASA and NOAA's global temperature report confirms what billions of people around the world experienced last year; we are facing a climate crisis. From extreme heat, to wildfires, to rising sea levels, we can see our Earth is changing." Noting that hundreds of millions of people around the world experienced extreme heat, NASA also affirmed that each month from June through December set a global record, and that July 2023 was the hottest month on Earth ever recorded.

Exacerbating the threats posed by the climate crisis, the killer heat sucking life from lungs worldwide also spawned what turned out to be the most devastating wildfire season on record in Canada and the U.S.A.

In 1989, Canada was confronted with what was the worst wildfire season on record at the time. That year more than 7.6 million hectares were consumed by the fires. During the 2023 wildfire season

---

22   On January 10, 2025 the World Meteorological Organization confirmed that 2024 was the hottest year on record. World Meteorological Organization website, 2025, https://wmo.int/news/media-centre/wmo-confirms-2024-warmest-year-record-about-155degc-above-pre-industrial-level

in Canada, however, some 16.5 million hectares of Canadian land including the forests, communities, and six people were incinerated by flames or choked out by smoke. That's more than four times the size of Estonia, and eight times the size of Israel, gone, melted and turned to ash.

"It's a Bird's World", *Arne Roosman,* charcoal on paper, 2021.

"It takes talent and silence to let and hear the Angels sing.", *Arne Roosman,* mixed media on paper, 2021.

"It takes talent and silence to let and hear the Angels sing."
- Arne Roosman

*There is no other definition of socialism valid for us
than that of the abolition of the exploitation of man by man.*
- Ernesto "Che" Guevara, 1965

SOCIALIST SWEDEN: A FIRST TASTE OF FREEDOM

From fleeing Keila and landing in Nazi-controlled Schwerin as a no-good, un-German traitor, to living in the Oxford DP camp near Lübeck, the concept of freedom has always seemed foreign to Arne. Living in Stockholm as a young man, he had his first real taste of what it felt like to be "free." For Arne, Socialist Sweden became somewhat of a beacon, a benchmark used to measure a government's level of sincerity when it comes to looking out for the best interests of the people who empower it. It was also in Stockholm, while protesting the Soviets' downing of two Swedish jets over international waters in the Baltic Sea, that Arne, as Aristotle would say, became a political animal.

"Sabres Drawn", *Arne Roosman,* charcoal on paper, 2014.

"An incident where Swedish commercial aircraft were shot down by Soviet Mig fighters over the Baltic Sea, if not, Swedish territorial waters.
This caused protesters by the thousands to gather at the Soviet Embassy in Stockholm.
Local constabulary on horses were employed to disperse, sabers drawn,
the still reasonably behaved multitude,
when black limos, slowly, at a funeral pace, with curtains drawn emerge from the embassy.
Madame Kollontay, who I believe was ambassador still at the time,
was pelted with a variety of projectiles: bottles, pop cans, apples, tomatoes.
Those on horseback moved in, slowly nudging the crowd, myself included, hot equine posteriors.
Now raw violence seemed to erupt.

A hero not.

I soon found myself on the retreat, if not on the run... a pacifist born.
That night of war I grew up.
That horrible game grown-ups play to please many gods,
be it clowns like Loki or pathetic, glorified Odin.
Godly image is bound to suffer. Ragnarok, ever beckoning in eternal darkness."

– Arne Roosman

Settling down in Sweden, sometimes called Svedala, The Dale Svea, The Mother of the ancient Germanic Tribe, the Swedes, Arne's feet were now planted firmly on solid ground, where the very pronunciation of his name had a new, but ancient ring. Papa Axel's advice to Arne on his 16th birthday: to pick up a trade. Arne did; he followed in his father's footsteps and began studying lithography. His Mother Helle's advice: "A book under every pillow. READ!" From Alois Senefelder to Axel Roosman, to Arne, he said they kept Latin alive by writing on stone. Lithographers, par excellence!

Traditionally, tradesmen, machinery, and chemistry of the printing trades relied on imports of all those from Germany, Switzerland, England, etc. but Arne was among a "new breed" of locally trained lithographers.

While in Stockholm Arne was immersed in some of the best and most influential art created by the poorly named 'Silent Generation.' He had a chance to see Nat King Cole perform at a hall that was filled to capacity. Arne said he only caught a glimpse of Nat performing, "Across a crowded room..." as the lyrics go, but he could hear the greatness of his voice perfectly.

On a night out in Stockholm with his brother Benny and his first of five wives, Arne said he got to witness the magic of Ella Fitzgerald on stage.

"Ella was but a few feet away, and she was really singing for us," Arne said.

On another evening in 1953, while taking in an opera with a friend, Arne said the performance was disrupted by a couple that was engaged in a spat a few rows behind them.

"I was happily enjoying the concert at the opera, when a few rows behind us, a couple started having a rather loud spat, all in good Yankee English. It was Frank Sinatra and Ava Gardiner having it out in public. Their visit to Sweden was front page news."

IN THE NEXT 100 YEARS

Around the time Arne was born, fascist forces throughout Europe and around the globe were mobilizing for war. By 1936, the people of Spain had become deeply divided, and many were looking towards fascism as a viable alternative form of government. In July of 1936, General Francisco Franco took part in a failed coup which ignited the Spanish Civil War.

It was in Guernica, a predominantly working-class town in the Basque region of northern Spain, where the world learned how far fascists were willing to go to gain power. To squash a political uprising in the town that was threatening his rise to power, on April 26, 1937, Franco recruited the Nazi German Luftwaffe's Condor Legion and the Fascist Italian Aviazione Legionaria to help his faction of Nationalist rebels take over the town by bombing Guernica from above.

As foreshadowing of the Second World War knocked at the door, Operation Rügen as it was called, would make history; not because of the 200–250 people who were killed in the raids on the Spanish City of Guernica, or the hundreds of others wounded, but because Operation Rügen was the world's first ever aerial saturation bombing (BBC 2007). It was quite an achievement in the human art of killing, but a much bigger step backwards on the road to peace.

Picasso's painting of the destruction in Guernica represents for Arne a new way of teaching people about the tangible horrors of war. More importantly, he said it inspired all those who saw it to

Words were not given to man in order to conceal his thoughts.
- Jose Saramago, 2000

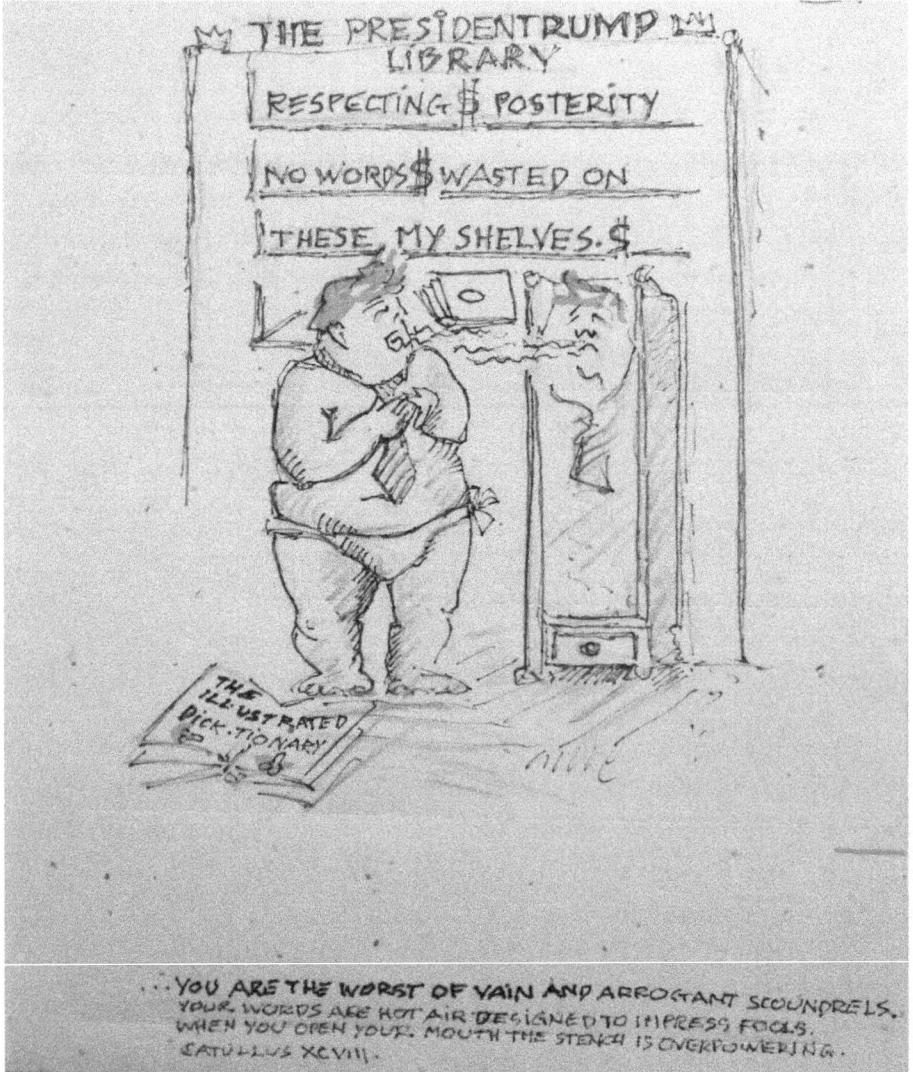

"Freedom of Thought", *Arne Roosman,* mixed media on paper, 2021.

think about the value of peace. To tell this story, the painter presents a mother screaming in pain as she holds her dead baby, a woman fleeing a burning house in terror, and a dead soldier, still clutching his broken sword. A bull, the symbol of Spain, watches over the carnage.

During a discussion regarding the power of art to inspire positive societal change, Arne told me that if he had enough energy, and years, and time, if he had another 100 years left, the focus of his painting would be promoting peace in a similar manner to how Pablo Picasso's Guernica does.

After Picasso finished the piece, Arne said it was sent on a tour of Europe. Fortunately for him, the first stop on the tour was at the new national museum in Stockholm. Still making sense of his life during wartime in the rearview mirror while he was living in Sweden, Arne stood before Picasso's Guernica; it echoed his childhood during the war. His firsthand experience of violence during wartime had shown him that peace is always a preferable state of existence.

"I was there," Arne said proudly. "When I went to see Guernica, I was so impressed. And I'm not even a Picasso fan. But in a way, Guernica connected with my young life."

Entering the new museum for the first time was a memorable moment for Arne. Describing those first steps into the gallery's womb of creativity, he said, "Going into the modern museum, you walked into, in plain language, a cunt. What they did for the entrance at the new national Museum in Stockholm was make it a vagina. We all come from there, so to see the art that we can create, we have to go back into the pussy. We have to go back inside to really appreciate art."

"Would you say that this was the first time you were inspired by another artist's art?"

"Well, it shocked me," Arne replied. "Guernica was such a new idea of how to speak on the canvas. Even the art world as we knew it was taken back. Everybody was both impressed, and the anti-modernists, well, they were shocked by him painting horses like

that with women screaming. But that's the pain of war. It's all depict-
ed there so well. So, when you see that painting live, and you have
ever been concerned about what art is all about, it is amazing. What
it does to you — and remember Nate, I am not a fan of Picasso —
from an intellectual point of view, you can't look away from Picasso.
He's one of the most important entities of that kind of endeavour.
It is like how some music just goes past your ears, and you can't take
it. You can't deny its existence, when it's not your thing. It can be so
much not your thing that you turn against it, but besides those intellectual considerations, I wish I were Picasso in a sense, from what he
put out."

"Well Arne, here's to Picasso!" I said, raising my drink. "And
the next 100 years!"

"Yeah! And the next Picasso!" Arne said. "I would not hesitate
to become another Picasso if I had another 100 years not by copying
him, but just letting myself go and not letting convention interfere
with my thought pattern, with my drifting into some intellectual
controversy, etc., etc. I wouldn't give a shit about what the world
would think I was doing. I would really work like Picasso. I would
do what I think should be done intellectually to open the eyes of the
millions who don't know how to look at life. Now I am a preacher,'"
he said, laughing.

One of the most valuable skills one must learn in life, Arne
said, is the ability to listen. Looking back on the past 92+ years of his
life, he said the sooner we learn to listen to others, the better off we
will be personally, and as a community.

"You have to listen. Not just to me, but to everybody that
you don't listen to usually. It's about time everyone started listening,
because the time has come where we are not alone. We are together
in this, and together we have kept on killing, killing, killing! It is together, now, our time to stay alive, and enjoy; to be, be, be! Not to be
'has beens' but to actually want to be. Not to live on past glory and
future promises, but live in the present, as it happens to come at us
as a payback for our giving, giving, giving."

"So you would ignore convention and just be in the moment,

and create with a purpose?"

"Yeah, like Picasso kissed them goodbye, and went his own way."

"That's a brave thing to do, Arne. Hell, just creating art and identifying as an artist takes courage. I have had a chance to interview a lot of artists and craftspeople over the years and many of them get kind of shy when I ask them how they became an artist."

"It can also be an excuse to say any kind of shit one wants," said Arne. "People will say, 'You're full of shit!' And I could say, 'No, I'm not full of shit, I'm an artist.' That very title gives me the freedom to do whatever I want! So, if politics is an art, then Trump is in the same boat, only it leaks."

HITCHING A RIDE ALONG THE RHINE

Arne's urge to travel grew stronger as he was becoming an adult. Exploring Sweden outside of Stockholm, he set out for the countryside with an older friend of his, Bengt Jallinder to visit the little Hamlet of Västerhaninge.

Bengt oversaw the local ambulance. Should someone die, Arne said Bengt would bring them back to his basement where he would do the embalming.

"We had movie nights in the same room," Arne said. "Bengt projected porn to our delight. We were surrounded by coffins, some closed, some open. Bone, rattling, ghosts, or were they rats making all that noise?"

"Lost at Sunset", *Arne Roosman,* mixed media on paper, 2021.

At one time, our past was the future.
Hand-in-hand with the present.
Words, words, then numbers.
Yesterday I was five, today I am six... 'Mummy!
When and where do numbers end?' he asked.
'Arne boy, ask Albert Einstein, he's got a number for a name.
If anybody, he should know.'
Years down the road when I hitchhike in Konrad Adenauer's new Germany,
I had 'Ein stein' of beer that was almost a litre.
The fascination with numbers brings about words,
and vice versa as Caesar would put it.
– Arne Roosman

"Numbers Talk", *Arne Roosman,* mixed media on paper, 2021.

Curiosity has always compelled Arne to explore and interpret his world. While living in Tungelsta, Arne explored his new-found freedom. Taking a train to the Danish capital of Copenhagen, he stuck out his thumb by the side of the road, with his sights set on the Rhine River. Once standing riverside, Arne said his plan was to hitchhike along the Rhine, until he reached his cousin Olaf the Optometrist's home near Heidelberg, Germany.

"Where's My Other Eye, Zuckerberg?!", *Arne Roosman,* mixed media on paper, 2021.

Urgent urging from upper Manhattan.
Give up on Sweden, the future is in America.
Your uncle and his patented, 'Dust brick',
now making waves on the Hudson River.
The factory, a jewel of accomplishment, says Auntie Magda.
So, I was off to the U.S. Embassy.
Who was I to argue?
In spite of these credits, my entry to the U.S. was refused.
— Arne Roosman

MISSING THE *MAASDAM*

Upon Arne's arrival at the U.S. Embassy, the ambassador surprised him by addressing him by his first name. This was not customary in Sweden, so it got his attention.

"Sorry Arne, the Estonian quota is way overdrawn, so you'll have to come back in a year or so," she told him.

Ready to make a move and unwilling to wait, he walked next door to the Canadian Embassy. He was served instantly. Within a few months, Arne was en route to Canada to begin the next chapter of his life.

"You know Arne, all these years of us shooting the shit, and I don't think we have ever talked about your voyage across the Atlantic to Canada. How was the trip?"

"Oh yeah. That's where I fell in love with what's-her-name," he said. "I never mentioned her?"

"No, not that I can recall," I said.

"Ho, ho! So much in love, eh. What a fucker I am," he laughed. "Well, we can't forget the Lady of the Atlantic. We better roll back to Sweden then, or young Arne will miss the *Maasdam* — the steamship that carried me to Canada — where I met Greta Olsen; a flying escort of gulls; a Sonnet in C major of dolphins, cutting waves between me and my distant new home in 'Oh, Canada!' See, aboard the *Maasdam* they had these seating arrangements, so everybody was sitting in pre-arranged seats. When the boat goes up and down, and up and down, and up and down, nobody sits... except Arne Roosman because he doesn't get seasick. As everybody else was out there puking into the ocean, I was just sitting there, when all of a sudden, there she was, Greta Olsen — a regular Scandinavian name. I started talking to her, and her Dad was a graphic artist in Los Angeles named Olsen. Greta was just on her way back from visiting relatives in Europe. So, I was talking to somebody who was an English speaker, but Swedish in descent. A typical American Swede, you know, not too bad at Swedish, but we were speaking English. I really fell for her because there was nothing really to do but fall in love with a nice woman. She was not the local beauty, but she was good looking, regular, middle class, and we had lots to talk about. She had been travelling all over Italy and Germany a lot, so we had all these connections. For a week, I was constantly with this one beautiful lady. Of course, every night when the ship wasn't moving too badly after supper, there was a band of professional musicians that played dance music. So, every night there was a dance, and people were dancing. The Master of Ceremonies, he instructed us, telling us how we would have a problem dancing because the movement of the boat doesn't stop. The only way you can handle dancing on the boat, he said, was to change your habitual dance steps. So, the dance step was like this: because the boat was constantly dipping one way and then the other way, back and forth, back and forth. 'Da, di, di, Da, di, di, Da'. The MC told us 'I can't do it now because of my back' but he told us you just stand there and hold your loved one, however you hold her, but stand with your legs apart. When your legs are apart, all you do is you use your legs, left and right, left and right, always keep your legs apart because that counteracts the movement of the boat. If you just dance normal, say like in a waltz with the short and the long, short and long, short and long, you will fall down on the short, because the boat will go with the long while you're going with the short. So that was Greta Olsen."

"Oh yeah. The Atlantic, she'll throw you around," I said, recalling how I nearly got myself tossed into the big stew from the upper deck of the MV Lyubov Orlova back in September of 2000. Running off on a tangent inspired by Arne's lucid description of the ocean's dance, I told him about how I was nearly thrown overboard, after I disobeyed the Captain's orders to stay below deck, while

276

crossing the turbulent waters of the Davis Strait between Greenland and Labrador.

I had found my way aboard an old Russian spy ship which was converted into a relatively small-scale, 105-passenger, ecotourism cruise ship, as part of a photography expedition retracing the Vikings' first known journey to North America some 2000 years earlier. Prior to leaving Kangerlussuaq, Greenland, we were told that it would take about 24 hours to reach Northern Labrador, and that the waters would be 'rough'. Looking back, I now realize they undersold this part of the voyage on the application.

The ship noticeably began swaying as the crew was preparing dinner. To prevent everything from sliding off the tables, the waitresses went around spraying the tablecloths with water. However, before they could even put the food out the Captain's voice came across the loudspeaker:

"We are going to be going through some very rough waters for the next while, so we have cancelled dinner. Everyone is to remain below deck in their cabins, until further notice."

Standing up from the table where I had taken a seat early for dinner, the ship dipped sharply to the right, knocking me off my feet and into one of the tables behind me. One of the waitresses spraying the tables had fallen during the roll as well, causing her to knock over the cleaning cart. Slowly, walking like I'd just polished off a bottle of rye, I made my way across the room to help her clean up. As I picked up the pieces of a smashed plate, another woman, who I assume was the manager came out and told us both to leave the mess and go to our bunks. I decided that before I went downstairs to ride out the long night ahead, strapped in my bunk, I would take a trip topside to snap a couple photos of the massive waves pummeling the vessel. Widening my stance, as I learned later Arne's dance instructor advised, I opened the door to the upper deck outside. Almost at the exact moment I stepped outside, the ship rolled violently again. Losing my footing, before I could blink, I was on my ass and sliding speedily toward the edge. If it wasn't for the bolt sticking up from the deck that snagged my sweater and gave me the moment that I needed to latch onto a life preserver affixed to the railing, that would have been it.

With my toes dangling over the Atlantic, I waited for the ship to roll in the other direction, so I could ride the momentum back to the door that was still propped open. Hanging onto the life preserver just in case, I waited for the right moment and let go.

Skating across the slippery surface of the deck on my ass, I crashed into the wall beside the door. As I latched onto the door handle, the ship rolled aggressively the other way again, preventing me from finding my feet. Literally hanging on for my life, I waited again for it to dip in the other direction. As it did, with all my strength I flung myself through the open doorway. Getting a hand on the frame, I quickly pulled myself back inside. Drenched in seawater and out of breath, shaking from the cold and the thought of my near untimely demise, I sat there on the inner deck with my back against the wall... grateful for loose bolts, well-placed life preservers, and doors that don't shut properly.

BIENVENUE AU CANADA, EH!

When Arne's ship, the *Maasdam*, landed in Halifax, Nova Scotia, he said goodbye to Greta, and continued on his way. Less than impressed with Halifax's vibe at the time, which Arne described as 'boring' and 'mundane', he headed west for Hamilton. It was in the Hammer where Arne's life would change forever.

In Hamilton, Arne said he befriended a community of Estonians that helped make him feel comfortable in his new home and country. Having taken his father's advice back in Sweden almost a decade earlier, by the age of 25, Arne had already established himself a reputation as a top-notch lithographer. As a skilled European lithographer living in Canada, he quickly found work with an outfit called Reid Press.

"It sounds like your time in Sweden, before you came to Canada, had a big impact on you, Arne."

"Well, 'the before' is sometimes very important, especially in our teens. It's in our teens that we sort of wake up to the real world and we have to learn a trade, we have to learn languages," Arne said. "I learned four, five, six, eight languages. I'm versed in four, but I have a love of the Italian. When I read something like Catch 22 or some other writer that puts in the whole sentences of Latin or Italian, or French, I'm still catching on because I have been reading so much. I've always been quite fascinated with languages. Really when I came to Canada I thought, 'Oh wow, I'm going to learn French!' I had a good understanding of French, because in Sweden

I was reading English literature, Max Brand, writer of Western bull shit. He was sort of my private English teacher. Every pocketbook that came with his name on the cover, I bought that book at the radio station in Stockholm, and I read Max Brand. That was my teacher. So, when I finally made a connection with the English, American Embassy in Stockholm, she asked me, 'where did you pick up English?' I said, 'From Max Brand.' I don't think she knew who I was talking about," Arne chuckled.

"When I came to Canada, I looked at the money and it was in two languages, I expected everybody to speak two languages. I was in Toronto, and there were all my new colleagues at the little shop in Hamilton, and I asked, 'Does anybody speak French here?' They said, 'No', 'No', 'No.' Nobody. I thought I'd be speaking French in no time. Yeah, that's how I picked up English. I thought I would be reading French on the train, mixing it with Max Brand. I had this French book with pictures, and I picked up all these glossaries of French, and I thought I could tie all this together in Canada."

"Not in Ontario, eh. I blame Doug Ford," I said, joking.

"Nope! Not in Ontario! I had to go all the way to Québec to 'speak-a-de' French. It's a rollercoaster world one grows up in from ski slopes to war machines. Then, inevitably one has to roll back the time machine, since so much gets lost in my eagerness to tell the story. The chemistry of people's hobbies were, as my Papa's, often close to living nature; a circus of collecting assorted insects, so my chemical was the 'don't touch' arsenic. Highly poisonous, Papa sprayed it on his beautifully assembled dead bugs to kill live ones, so they would not molest the assembly of the has been. Insects, it is well known, have somewhat of a Cabalistic nature. More chemistry was strewn into my trade-to-be; lithography, writing on stone, which evolved from Senefelder's genius to the world of Kodak. Into all this gets sucked, yours truly. Happy to have an outlet for his artistic abilities. A beginning that has followed me since my teens and has no end in sight."

Later in his career Arne had a chance to meet with Ontario's current Premier Doug Ford to try to get a contract with his printing company. Surprisingly, when he presented his company's credentials to Ford, he was abruptly shown the door. Shocked by Ford's rudeness, Arne said he remembers their encounter that day well.

"The Fords had a big printing company making labels or something, so I went in on behalf of our company to try and get us a contract. When I was called into his office, I was ready to give him our pitch. Right away he asked me if we were a union shop. Believing he would think that was a good thing, I proudly reassured him that we were. But I was wrong. He immediately stood up and said, 'Get the fuck out of here! I don't deal with you fucking Union guys!' I couldn't believe how rude he was."

"But now he says he's 'For the People!' He just doesn't mention which people. He must mean those buddies of his that he was trying to sell the Greenbelt to," I said.

"Well, he's definitely not talking about the workers," Arne said.

As for love, one cannot take it lightly.
One's affections get crowded.
My heart ready to burst from all the pain there is at my window,
by what is going on down the street.
The people's idea and ideals can remain on the cross,
the skeletal mysteries of the crucified holiness,
to inspire artists well into the future.
Praise the artist that keeps the dead alive!
A Halo, if faith you need.
– Arne Roosman

HAND IN HAND

It was through Arne's Estonian friends in Hamilton that he met, or more accurately, reunited with the love of his life, and soon to be mother of his two children, Liina Mora.

"Portrait of Liina", *Arne Roosman*, oil on canvas, 1961.

"I met Liina in 1957 on New Years Eve," Arne said, lighting up with a different kind of twinkle in his eye than I was used to seeing. "But it turned out that I had already met her 10 years earlier, in 1947, only I didn't know who she was. I didn't even see her, because she was five years younger than I was. Back in the camp I was almost 14, so I wasn't looking at an eight-year-old. I was 14 so I was looking at all the 14's. So back then there was this eight-year-old right in our house with my sister, who never paid attention to me either."

"Which of your sisters was she friends with?"

"Marit, the one who is here in Canada."

"So they became friends after the war?

"Yeah, in the DP camp in Lübeck, Germany."

"How did the two of you cross paths again?"

"We met again— although we didn't really meet in Germany — I met her in Toronto at the New Year's Dance at what was then a big entertainment venue down on Lakeshore Boulevard... At this celebration, a friend of mine from the Estonian community in the DP Camp —Camp Oxford —Peter, invited me to sit at his table. There was this young lady of 19, and there was me of 24. She was there with another chap as company, but it seemed that she was not particularly engaged with him, because she just didn't give a shit. She just turned around and we had a conversation, blah, blah, blah. It was a round table. There was me, Liina and her escort — myself solo — there were a few other solos. There were about eight of us at one of those big round tables. Then, at 12 o'clock the announcement of the New Year came the waltz from the orchestra. The waltz would be a Viennese waltz, so then you had the privilege to ask a girl for the first dance of the year. That was the big moment of the evening, and I asked Liina, and yes, she came, and we danced the first waltz of the year, a Viennese waltz... 'Um-duck-duck-Um-duck-duck...' Kaiser-Walzer, it's one of the famous Strauss waltzes. So, there we were, waltzing along on the waves of the Danube."

Liina lived in Hamilton, just like me, so I asked her whether I could have a date with her in Hamilton— go to the movies or whatever— she said 'Yes!' She had no steady company in Hamilton, but she lived with other Estonians. In those days if you were Latvian,

"Dancing the Flamenco", *Arne Roosman*, oil on canvas, 2013.

you lived in a Latvian house, same with Estonians because there was always that ethnic connection that gave you a place to socialize."

"It's so nice to learn how people often establish a community to support each other when they immigrate to another country," I said. "So how was the first date?"

"Toronto on New Year's Eve was a coincidence; it was not a date. We just happened to be there at the same time. A couple of weeks later, I got her phone number, and we made a date. So, we met, and she came upstairs into my flat—we were going to the movies or whatever—so she was getting ready for whatever we were going to do. It was not that she had a date with me at my place where we were going to bed together; no, no, no. She just came up because I was getting ready to go to the movies. That's when she saw the picture and said, 'Oh, I know this girl! That's Marit!' A year later I asked her to get married. On the 13th of December, which is St. Lucia Day in Sweden—which we celebrate with the candles on the girls' heads—that's when we arranged it with the Estonian Church in Hamilton. So that's when we got married, on the 13th of December in 1957. The wedding guests, they were mostly the ones there on New Year's Eve. It was the same crowd, and we all got together again, just like on January 1st, except this time we were celebrating our wedding."

"Wow! What a nice story, Arne! What are the chances?"

While Arne and Liina lived in Hamilton, they welcomed their first daughter Anne into the world on November 11, 1959. Liina became pregnant again and within a year and a half from Anne's arrival, she gave birth to their second daughter, Rebecca. Living in Toronto by this time, Arne became more active with the Lithographers' Union. At any given time, Arne said the Union would have anywhere from 75 to 125 active members. When the Union got together on special occasions, he said they would celebrate at the Town Hall with a multi-course dinner paraded through the candlelit dining room by waiters dressed all in white. Painting a picture of the joy and luxuriousness of these gatherings, Arne said they "...had a choice of Renat Brännvin, or cognac, and wine, both red or white. The music was as Swedish as the herring, the turkey, the dessert... the huge mosaic of Mother Svea—Mother of all the Swedes—smiling at

286

us from her heavenly appearance on the central wall reaching to the heavens."

In Toronto, Arne's career as a lithographer took off. In high demand, the young family appreciated the cultural experiences available in the city. Arne said they always loved spending time in Nature. When I asked Arne how he and Liina ended up moving north and landing near Bancroft, he said they were introduced to the area by some of his Estonian buddies from "the big city" who liked to go camping near Combermere. Falling in love with the natural beauty and peace of the region, Arne and Liina started driving north to escape the busy pace of life in the city whenever they could get away. It was on one of these camping expeditions, he said that they discovered the property on Monck Road near Cardiff where they would eventually retire in 1988.

WOLVES AT THE DOOR

Anytime Monck Road came up, it was as if I had located a treasure chest full of fond memories that had slipped into the recesses of the mind. Staring into space as if probing the depths of the cosmos, Arne recalled celebrating one of his birthdays there with his family.

"You know what it's like here, in March there might just be a blizzard to deal with. You never know. When [daughter] Rebecca was still living in Canada, we had a little get together for my birthday on Monck Road, yeah, and there was a snowstorm like you wouldn't believe. Rebecca went outside in the storm with a Mexican shawl around her neck and did a dance in the snow."

"It sounds as if that place, Monck Road, was a special place," I said, imagining the connection he must have established with the land over the nearly two decades he lived there.

"It was a very nice place. There were bears coming right up to the house. Wolves too! The wolves came right to the door one night when I was designing the Canadian whisky book. They looked right in the window to see the dogs. But the worst of course was the bear. One day when we had an artist friend staying with us overnight—he was sort of a chain-smoker, so he was outside smoking all the time—he had a close call with one and almost didn't even know it. We used to walk with our dogs from our little house down towards Cardiff. There's a very steep hill going down into Cardiff where we would turn around with our dogs. So, this one day when I'm coming back from the field with the dogs and reach the top of the hill, I see

"Wolves at the Door", *Arne Roosman*, charcoal on paper, 2021.

a bear crossing right at our house, less than 100 feet away from where I see him. I know this bear is going to turn around if he doesn't find anything exciting on that side of the road; and if he turned around, he was going to go right back behind our house. As I'm approaching, I see the bear and I am talking loudly and singing, because I see my friend by the door smoking, and he doesn't even know the bear is right there! Luckily, he heard me singing and took off."

"Monck Road", *Arne Roosman,* charcoal on paper, 1994.

UNCLE GUSTAF

"Now that bears have slid into our conversation, Uncle Gustav, of the Boesberg clan, deserves at least a few lines, most likely a hell of a lot more," said Arne. "It was not uncommon in the 18th and 19th centuries to have characters like Gustav pop up in families and history at an early age. At age 14 he was a correspondent with the Estonian, German, and Russian publications, each written in their own language. He was well-travelled in both countries, a master chess player with some competitive credits."

"So where do the Bears come in?"

"Well Nate, after some worries about tuberculosis in Switzerland, he took off wrestling bears to make a living at the mature age of 19."

"Really?" I asked, unsure if he was joking.

"Yeah. Apparently, he would put the Bears in a full Nelson," he replied sincerely. "He was part of a travelling circus. In March 2023 they opened a museum in Estonia in Gustav Boesberg's name. I was supposed to visit the opening, but my impediment, wheelchair, backache, well, you've seen me trying to get around. Gustav's fame would have reached me had he lived until 1932. I think I missed him by about six years. His brother, my grandpa Joseph has written and illustrated a beautiful family story, which touches on Gustav."

"Uncle Gustav Versus 'The Bear'", *Arne Roosman*, charcoal and conte on paper, 2021.

"I should mention our quartet of sisters again – Ingrid, Eva, Marit, and Signe Maria – as they deserve due attention," he continued. "Our family, rather recent settlers in Sweden, did sort of call at home, but the girls found their professions, went back to school, and did a lot of travelling all over Europe. They found sweethearts, and one married. The youngest, Signe Maria, was rather restless, had a child, a boy. She studied art and became quite proficient in her pursuits. Her focus seemed to be on getting to know people of worth and talent; and they had to be a somebody," he said. "Like the Redgraves in England, and Michael Meyer, author of stage and memoirs of the cultured famous like Ibsen, Strindberg. She eventually settled in Kent of Britain, where she and her husband Michael had a daughter. Michael was a Swedish son, who settled in Norway, then in England, where I visited them.

"She had not seen me for all the years I had been in Canada," he said. "She had grown by several inches. She was now at six-foot-one-inch and me at 1.75 metres. She burst out, 'Arne! You have shrunk!'"

While there, Arne said they introduced their daughters Anne and Rebecca to their grandparents and Uncle Benny. Then, he said it was off to Uppsala and Axel's brother Max, the prolific artist and ceramicist, and his wife Auntie Trudy of the Baltic German Fedder Clan.

"Arne's Daughter Rebecca (20 years old)", photograph, 1984.

"To see a World in a Grain of Sand
And a Heaven in a Wild Flower,
Hold Infinity in the palm of your hand
And Eternity in an hour."
- William Blake, 1863

"Once Upon a Time Many Moons Ago", *Arne Roosman*, mixed media
on paper, 2014.

UNFORGETTABLE LOVE

About 50 years after they were married, Liina took ill with a mysterious ailment that Arne said still today has no name. In all North America, he said there were only around 300 other people dealing with the same illness.

"Liina was taken to different hospitals — Belleville, Scarborough, Peterborough — and they were testing this and testing that. They didn't know what to do," Arne said. "Eventually she wasn't able to function anymore. That's when I sold the house in Cardiff; sold the house and moved to Bancroft, to that beautiful place on the York River. That's where I did a lot of the mural artwork. That was sort of the end of Liina because she had to stay in different hospitals and never moved into the place on the river. Liina was now staying at the Hastings Manor in Bancroft, and I was living [close by] down on the river."

While living in this space, over the course of six months, Arne created a huge mural depicting the history of the York River in Bancroft, which was installed in June of 2014 on the riverside wall of a building on Bridge Street West.

"After two or three years of that strange situation, I visited her on New Year's Eve 2015. As it was my habit reading to her— not that she was conscious, as she didn't even know I was real or she didn't appear to be alert, she didn't appear to be with it, she just lay there with her eyes open— and I was reading our usual Christmas reading by Dickens, *A Christmas Carol*. I was at chapter nine, I think,

"Liina's Passport Photo - 19 Years Old", photograph, 1960.

and I noticed that she was not paying attention, she was somewhere else, eyes wide open, laying there. On my way to visit her that night on New Year's Eve, on the radio they announced on the news while I was driving that Natalie Cole, the daughter of Nat King Cole, had just died of cancer. I think she was 65 or something, she wasn't that old. When I left Liina that night, I told her, 'Look, I wish that you could follow me now, but when I was driving here to see you Natalie Cole just died... so Liina, why don't you catch up with her.' That's what I told Liina, but there was no response. When I got home, the phone rings — I got it within a couple rings — and it was the Manor. They said, 'Arne, Liina is dying.' Then they said, 'From our experience, she won't have many hours, she's going.' I said, 'Could I make it back to see her off?' And they said, 'No, you won't make it.' So, 10 minutes later they phoned again and said she died. In my books, she caught up with Natalie Cole, because I told her, 'Run up!' And she did. And it could be quite true, because when people are in a dying situation, passing down this world, they just might connect, but we don't know because they aren't able to tell us. She might have thought, 'What a good idea. Why don't I die right now and catch up with Natalie?' Because we both like Natalie Cole. I mean, who doesn't? So that's the story and that's the end. Then we had some ceremonies and whatever it takes."

"A Touch of Jazz: Natalie Cole", *Arne Roosman*, charcoal on paper, 2019.

Did you hear about the rose that grew from a crack in the concrete?
Proving nature's law is wrong, it learned to walk without having feet.
Funny, it seems, but by keeping its dreams, it learned to breathe fresh air.
Long live the rose that grew from concrete when no one else even cared.
- Tupac Shakur, 1989

LIFE FINDS A WAY

It was Saturday, June 17, 2023, around 11 a.m. when I paused for a moment to reflect on what I had learned and was learning from Arne as we navigated the creative process together. I remember the day vividly because there was a thick haze of wildfire smoke weighing heavily on the air over Bancroft. This poison entering our lungs was but a hint of the heavy burden we are still choosing to leave behind for our children, children's children, and all our loved ones for at least the foreseeable future...

On this morning Arne and I were running a few errands in Bancroft before driving south for a community art exhibition at the Christ Church in Toronto displaying some of his artwork, along with works by several other members of the Roosman family. Wearing masks – not because of COVID-19, but because the air tasted like fire, we rolled through town as if we were on a mission. Our objectives that morning: 1) Stop by the pharmacy to pick up drugs; 2) Visit our friends at the local cannabis dispensary and grab a bottle of CBD oil to ease Arne's pain; 3) the grocery store; and 3) Pay a few bills and/or rob the bank.

The pharmacy was in and out, as the order had been filled over the phone ahead of time. Same with the cannabis shop. Arne's arthritis had been causing him a lot of pain for almost six months, so I recommended that he give CBD a try. Whenever Arne talks about his pain, he advises me:

"Live forever, but don't get old in the process."

After a couple weeks of experimenting, Arne said he noticed that the pain he had been experiencing was significantly reduced. This was especially evident at bedtime, when he noticed that he hadn't "slept so well in a long time."

Motoring through the grocery store as quickly as possible, we headed over to the bank, our last stop for the day. We joked about our bandit masks and me keeping the car running while he went in to clean out the safe.

Sitting there in the car, waiting with the engine running for Arne to come out with the loot, I thought about all the things we talked about and how these conversations have influenced and moved me in such a profound way.

There is no way I could write down all that Arne has taught me, but here is the one "most important thing": the value of spending time with those you love and respect. There is no way I could ever put a price tag on the moments and stories we have shared. Our exchange, and our friendship has taught me the great value of truly paying attention to what matters most. It has also shown me just how much there is to learn when we focus our time and energy on getting to know one another on a deeper than surface level.

Through Arne's art he has proved to me the power of creativity to inspire positive change when art emerges from the soul. In telling me about the challenges he faced as an immigrant and a child during wartime, he displayed for me the value of compassion and cooperation in the face of chaos.

"We must never stop questioning the divine!" Arne would say. "Never stop questioning!"

At the moment Arne's words entered my mind, the front door of the bank swung open and there he was. Stepping out to give him a hand, I opened the car door and took his bag. As he was getting back into the car, Arne suddenly stopped, stood up straight and then pointed his cane at two dandelions that had pushed their way up through a tiny crack in the pavement.

"Well, isn't that something," he said under his breath. "Life finds a way."

"What's that Arne? I asked.

"Life finds a way," he said. "It always finds a way."

"D For Dandelion", *Arne Roosman,* oil on canvas, 2023.

"Photo of Latte and Arne in his studio", Photograph by *N. Smelle*, 2021.

ARTIST'S EPILOGUE

A wingless angel, an angel, nevertheless;
hovering in my dreamscape of miserable years in DP camps,
of bread and no butter, pea, soup, corn soup, no soup.
Malnourished body carrying pimples in itchy armpits.
Then, leaving the classic "liberators" behind in the devastated Germany,
their field of conquest.
Meanwhile, my angel had grown wings,
transformed into the maid of Haninge in however neutral Sveadala.
Then, oh, Canada, the restless settles his wings defeathered.
The mind at rest.
Tears of sunshine, dew, fully keeping green,
green and flowers growing on many a grave.
Love given and much received.
Held in an angel's arms.

"Inspiration", *Arne Roosman,* mixed media on paper, 2021.

BIBLIOGRAPHY

"9 Minutes, 29 Seconds: Derek Chauvin Trial Opens with Full Video of George Floyd's Killing". *Democracy Now.* March 30, 2021. https://www.democracynow.org/2021/3/30/derek_chauvin_trial

Aggarwal, Mithil; Jett, Jennifer. "Hamas chief Ismail Haniyeh killed in Israeli airstrike in Iran, Hamas says". *NBC.* July 30, 2024. www.nbcnews.com/news/world/hamas-chief-ismail-haniyeh-killed-israeli-airstrike-iran-hamas-says-rcna164425

"ALLIED FIREBOMBING ON HAMBURG, DRESDEN, AND TOKYO". *Stanford Computer Science.* 2007. https://cs.stanford.edu/people/eroberts/courses/ww2/projects/firebombing/websitehamburg1.htm

Alfonseca, Kiara. "So-called 'Don't Say Gay' rules expanded through 12th grade in Florida". *ABC News.* April 19, 2023. https://abcnews.go.com/Politics/called-dont-gay-rules-expanded-12th-grade-florida/story?id=98691183

Angus, Charlie. "Pierre Poilievre's 19 Room Mansion - Lifestyles of the Rich and Famous (Ottawa edition)". *YouTube.* May 27, 2023. https://www.youtube.com/watch?v=A6ZHAw4k1Zg

Arasu, Sibi. "Study finds rains that led to deadly Indian landslides were made worse by climate change". *AP News.* Aug. 13, 2024. https://apnews.com/article/climate-change-wayanad-kerala-india-landslides-rainfall-a4b17a66d4ad74ba949b4102f9eafb87

At Liberty Podcast. "10 Years of #BlackLivesMatter: Progress and Backlash." *American Civil Liberties Union.* July 13, 2023. https://www.aclu.org/podcast/blacklivesmatter-progress-and-backlash

Bardan, Roxana. "NASA Analysis Confirms 2023 as Warmest Year on

Record". *NASA.* January 12, 2024. www.nasa.gov/news-release/nasa-analysis-confirms-2023-as-warmest-year-on-record/

Bardan, Roxana. "Temperatures Rising: NASA Confirms 2024 Warmest Year on Record". *NASA.* January 10, 2025. www.nasa.gov/news-release/temperatures-rising-nasa-confirms-2024-warmest-year-on-record/

Bauder, David; Riccardi, Nicholas. "Tucker Carlson's scorn for Trump revealed in defamation lawsuit filings". *PBS Newshour.* March 8, 2023. https://www.pbs.org/newshour/politics/tucker-carlsons-scorn-for-trump-revealed-in-defamation-lawsuit-filings

"BERLIN FALLS AND 1,000,000 SURRENDER IN ITALY: Dramatic news last night points to early end of Nazi's phony war". *London Daily Express.* May 2, 1945.

Black Elk; Brown, J. E. *The sacred pipe: Black Elk's account of the seven rites of the Oglala Sioux.* University of Oklahoma Press. 1953.

Blake, William. "Auguries of Innocence". *Poems,* ed. Dante Gabriel Rossetti 1863. www.poetryfoundation.org/poems/43650/auguries-of-innocence

Bohannon, Molly. "Trump Rally Speaker Tony Hinchcliffe Calls Puerto Rico 'Floating Island Of Garbage'—Campaign, GOP Lawmakers React." *Forbes.* 28 October 2024. https://www.forbes.com/sites/mollybohannon/2024/10/27/trump-rally-speaker-calls-puerto-rico-floating-island-of-garbage-campaign-says-joke-doesnt-reflect-trumps-views/

Borger, Julia; Kierszenbaum, Quique; Christou, William. "Israel launches 'pre-emptive' strikes on Lebanon as Hezbollah fires drones and rockets". *The Guardian.* August 25, 2024. https://www.theguardian.com/world/article/2024/aug/25/israel-pre-emptive-strikes-lebanon-huge-hezbollah-drone-and-rocket-attack

Bruce, Mary; Hutzler, Alexandra; Wang, Selina. "Harris officially names Tim Walz as vice presidential running mate". *ABC News.* August 6, 2024. https://abcnews.go.com/Politics/harris-poised-pick-tim-walz-vice-presidential-running/story?id=112241182

"Buffalo shooting suspect says his motive was to prevent 'eliminating the white race'". *The Associate Press.* June 16, 2022. https://www.npr.

org/2022/06/16/1105776617/buffalo-shooting-suspect-says-his-motive-was-to-prevent-eliminating-the-white-ra

"Burkina Faso massacre survivor describes bloodshed in trenches". *Reuters.* Aug. 31, 2024. https://www.reuters.com/world/africa/i-saw-horrible-things-burkina-faso-massacre-survivor-describes-bloodshed-2024-08-30/

Burroughs, William S. *The Cat Inside.* Grenfell Press. 1986

Callan, Isaac; D'Mello, Collin. "What did Doug Ford say about the Greenbelt? A timeline of the premier's promises". *Global News.* May 12, 2023. www.globalnews.ca/news/9694836/ontario-greenbelt-promise-timeline/

"Canada's record-breaking wildfires in 2023: A fiery wake-up call". *Government of Canada.* August 19, 2024. https://natural-resources.canada.ca/simply-science/canadas-record-breaking-wildfires-2023-fiery-wake-call/25303

"CDC Museum COVID-19 Timeline". *Center for Disease Control.* 2023. www.cdc.gov/museum/timeline/covid19.html

Churchwell, Sarah. *Behold, America: The Entangled History of 'America First' and 'the American Dream'.* Basic Books. 2018. https://www.amazon.com/Behold-America-Entangled-History-American/dp/1541673409

Clayton, Abene; Yang, Maya. "Dick Cheney confirms he will vote for Kamala Harris, saying no 'greater threat' to U.S. than Donald Trump – as it happened". *The Guardian.* September 6, 2024. https://www.theguardian.com/us-news/live/2024/sep/06/trump-harris-us-election?filterKeyEvents=false&page=with%3Ablock-66daf2628f08a9d0891e9540

Cohen, Marshall. "Elon Musk's daily $1 million giveaway to registered voters could be illegal, experts say". *CNN.* October 21, 2024. https://www.cnn.com/2024/10/20/politics/elon-musk-voter-giveaway-legal-questions/index.html

Cohen, Sacha Baron. Nov. 21, 2019. *Anti-Defamation League.* "Sacha Baron Cohen's Keynote Address at ADL's 2019 Never Is Now Summit on Anti-Semitism and Hate". https://www.adl.org/resources/news/sacha-baron-cohens-keynote-address-adls-2019-never-now-summit-anti-semitism-and-hate

Coletta, Amanda. "'Significant element' from U.S. involved in self-described 'Freedom Convoy' in Canada, official says". *The Washington Post*. February 2, 2022. .https://www.washingtonpost.com/world/2022/02/02/freedom-convoy-alberta-blockade-vaccine-mandate-protests/

Coon, Gene L.; Wilber, Carey. "Star Trek: Space Seed". *NBC*. February 27, 1967.

Fowler, Stephen. "Trump attacks Kamala Harris' racial identity at Black journalism convention". *NPR*. July 31, 2024. https://www.npr.org/2024/07/31/nx-s1-5059091/donald-trump-nabj-interview

"Freedom Convoy, Pat King talks bullets and race". *YouTube*. February 9, 2022. https://www.youtube.com/watch?v=f6GBPmtjh34

Gabbatt, Adam; Pilkington, Ed. "Trump fills Madison Square Garden with anger, vitriol and racist threats". *The Guardian*. October 28, 2024. https://www.theguardian.com/us-news/2024/oct/27/trump-madison-square-garden-rally

"Gas Ration, Quarterly Basis: No Hoarding Coupons From One Period to Next". *The Bancroft Times*. December 18, 1940.

"Germany shooting: 'Far-right extremist' carried out shisha bars attacks". February 20, 2020. *BBC News*. https://www.bbc.com/news/world-europe-51567971

Gilmore, Rachel. "Poilievre leads march of convoy protesters beside man with far-right extremist ties". *Global News*. June 30, 2022. https://globalnews.ca/news/8959365/canada-day-convoy-james-topp-far-right-pierre-poilievre/

"GIs get Hitler's Beer Hall". *The Bancroft Times*. August 16, 1945.

Gorman, Amanda. *Call Us What We Carry: Poems*. New York, Random House. 2021.

Guevara, Ernesto 'Che'. "Speech at the Second Economic Seminar of Afro-Asian Solidarity". February 24, 1965. https://www.marxists.org/archive/guevara/1965/02/24.htm

Habermas, Jürgen. *Religion and Rationality: Essays on Reason, God & Modernity*. Wiley. 2014.

"Arne at Studio Dreamshare", Photo by *Cameron Dreamshare*, October 5th, 2020.

Hamza, Assiya. "One year of war in Gaza: The key dates in the Israel-Hamas conflict". *France 24*. October 6, 2024. https://www.france24.com/en/middle-east/20241006-one-year-of-war-in-gaza-the-key-dates-in-the-israel-hamas-conflict

Helmore, Edward. "George Santos's weirdest lies revisited as he pleads guilty to fraud". *The Guardian*. August 19, 2024. www.theguardian.com/us-news/article/2024/aug/19/george-santos-weirdest-lies

Hemingway, Ernest. "Notes on the Next War". *Esquire*. September 1, 1935. https://classic.esquire.com/article/1935/9/1/notes-on-the-next-war

Hemingway Jaynes, Cristen. "80 Million People in U.S. Under Air Quality Alerts as Canada's Wildfire Smoke Swings South Again". *EcoWatch*. June 28, 2023. https://www.ecowatch.com/canada-wildfire-smoke-us-air-quality.html

"HITLER DEAD". *The Stars and Stripes (Paris edition)*. May 2, 1945. https://en.m.wikipedia.org/wiki/File:Stars_%26_Stripes_%26_Hitler_Dead2.jpg

"Hitler Quotes." *Gordon State College*. Accessed February 20, 2025. https://ptfaculty.gordonstate.edu/jmallory/index_files/page0508.htm

"Hitler's not going to teach my children!" Ad. *The Bancroft Times*. May 28, 1942.

Hodge, Nathan. "Assad's fall is huge blow for Putin, highlighting fragility of his own rule". *CNN*. December 9, 2024. https://edition.cnn.com/2024/12/09/europe/syria-russia-bashar-al-assad-analysis-intl-hnk/index.html

Hoffman, Riley. "READ: Harris-Trump presidential debate transcript". *ABC News*. September 10, 2024. https://abcnews.go.com/Politics/harris-trump-presidential-debate-transcript/story?id=113560542

Holmes, Kristen; Millar, John; Sullivan, Kate; Perez, Evan; Herb, Jeremy. "Trump is safe following shooting at Florida golf course; suspect detained". *CNN*. September 15, 2024. www.cnn.com/2024/09/15/politics/donald-trump-safe-shots/index.html

"HOSTILITIES CEASE WITH JAPAN'S SURRENDER: Nearly Six Years of War Ends With Capitulation of Japan". *The Bancroft Times*. August 16, 1945.

Howard, Andrew. "Suggesting 'nine barrels shooting' at Cheney, Trump reverts to violent rhetoric". *Politico*. November 1, 2024. https://www.politico.com/news/2024/11/01/cheney-trump-firing-squad-threats-are-how-dictators-destroy-free-nations-00186707

Huxley, Aldous. The Olive Tree. *The New Yorker*. 1937. https://archive.org/details/olivetreeooooaldo

"I'm a Free Man" Ad. *The Bancroft Times*. October 8, 1942.

Ingram, Julia; Reilly, Steve. "Elon Musk spends $277 million to back Trump and Republican candidates". *CBS News*. December 6, 2024. https://www.cbsnews.com/news/elon-musk-277-million-trump-republican-candidates-donations/

"Israeli strikes on Beirut and Tehran could intensify a regional war". *The Economist*. August 1, 2024. www.economist.com/middle-east-and-africa/2024/07/31/israeli-strikes-on-beirut-and-tehran-could-intensify-a-regional-war

Johnson, Hiram. "Senate speech". 1918. www.senate.gov/artandhistory/history/common/generic/Classic_Speeches.htm

Karl, Jonathan. "Donald Trump's history with Adolf Hitler and his Nazi writings." *ABC News*. December 20, 2023. https://abcnews.go.com/Politics/donald-trumps-history-adolf-hitler-nazi-writings-analysis/story?id=105810745

Kasekamp, Andres. "Fascism by Popular Initiative: The Rise and Fall of the Vaps Movement in Estonia." *Brill*. November 23, 2015. https://brill.com/view/journals/fasc/4/2/article-p155_5.xml?language=en

Kierkegaard, Søren. Garden City, N.Y.: Doubleday (1959). *Either/Or*. 1843.

King Jr., Martin Luther. "Where Do We Go from Here: Chaos or Community?". New York: Harper and Row. 1967

Kiyagan, Askin. "Far-right party founded by Nazis favorite in Austria's Sunday election". *Anadolu Agency*. September 29, 2024. https://www.aa.com.tr/en/europe/far-right-party-founded-by-nazis-favorite-in-austria-s-sunday-election/3341803#

Klug, Foster. "What to know about South Korea's martial law and the impeachment vote threatening its president". *The Associated Press*. December 12, 2024. https://apnews.com/article/south-korea-martial-law-north-korea-emergency-b310df4fece42c27051f58b8951f346f

Kormann, Carolyn. "Through the Smoke: Why Maui Burned". *The New Yorker*. November 6, 2023. https://www.newyorker.com/magazine/2023/11/06/maui-wildfire-response-recovery

Kulkarni, Akshay. "A look back at the 2021 B.C. wildfire season". *CBC News*. October 4, 2021. https://www.cbc.ca/news/canada/british-columbia/bc-wildfires-2021-timeline-1.6197751

"LATEST: SUICIDE BY HITLER, GOEBBELS". *London Daily Express*. May 2, 1945.

Lederer, Edith M. "At least $1 billion needed to avert famine in Somalia, U.N. says". *PBS News*. September 1, 2022. https://www.pbs.org/newshour/world/at-least-1-billion-needed-to-avert-famine-in-somalia-u-n-says

Lemire, Johnathan. "Elon Musk is President." *The Atlantic*. February 3, 2025. www.theatlantic.com/politics/archive/2025/02/president-elon-musk-trump/681558/

Lewis, Helen. "Donald Trump's Latest Violent Fantasy: The former president muses about reporters getting shot". *The Atlantic*. November 3, 2024.https://www.theatlantic.com/politics/archive/2024/11/trump-fantasizes-about-reporters-being-shot/680514/

Lowell, Hugo. Sept. 26, 2024. *The Guardian*. "Trump ground game operation now largely run by Elon Musk-backed group". https://www.theguardian.com/us-news/2024/sep/26/trump-voter-turnout-elon-musk-pac

Macdonald, Dwight. *Masscult and Midcult: Essays Against the American Grain*. New York Review Books Collection. January 1, 1962.

Margaritoff, Marco. "Elon Musk Endorses Germany's Far-Right Party: 'Only The AFD Can Save Germany'." *HuffPost*. December 20, 2024 www.huffpost.com/entry/elon-musk-endorses-germanys-far-right-party-only-the-afd-can-save-germany_n_6765ad00e4b018cc0607413c

Matthews, James. "Neo-Nazi group salutes Hitler in Florida demonstration". *Sky News*. September 5, 2023. https://news.sky.com/video/neo-nazi-group-salutes-hitler-in-florida-demonstration-12955833

Maza, Cristina. "Trump Will Start the End of the World, Claim Evangelicals Who Support Him." *Newsweek.* January 12, 2018. https://www.newsweek.com/trump-will-bring-about-end-worldevangelicals-end-times-779643

McCann Ramirez, Nikki. "So ... What's With This Rumor That J.D. Vance Had Sex With a Couch?" Rolling Stone. July 25, 2024. www.rollingstone.com/politics/politics-news/jd-vance-couch-sex-rumor-explained-1235068142/

McGrath, Matt. "Scientists say climate change made Spanish floods worse". *BBC News.* October 30, 2024. https://www.bbc.com/news/articles/c98eylqego60

"Misinformation" cartoon. *The Bancroft Times.* January 8, 1942.

Mowat, Farley. *Never cry wolf.* Austin, Holt, Rinehart and Winston. 2000.

Mureithi, Carlos. "Death toll from Ethiopia landslides could reach 500, UN agency says". *The Guardian.* July 25, 2024. www.theguardian.com/world/article/2024/jul/25/death-toll-from-ethiopia-landslides-could-reach-500-un-agency-says.

"Nagasaki after the bomb" photos. *The Bancroft Times.* August 16, 1945.

Nasser, Shanifa; Blum, Benjamin. "Canada's 1st 'presumptive' case of coronavirus found in Toronto". *CBC News.* January 25, 2020. https://www.cbc.ca/news/canada/toronto/canada-1st-case-coronavirus-toronto-1.5440760

"NAZI RADIO ANNOUNCES: HITLER DEAD 'FELL IN COMMAND POST' ADMIN. DOENITZ NAMED HEAD OF REICH, ARMY". *New York's Daily News,* May 2, 1945.

Ndegwa, Anna; McDonald, Susan. "Hate Crimes in Canada". *Government of Canada.* November 15, 2023. https://www.justice.gc.ca/eng/rp-pr/cj-jp/victim/rd16-rr16/p1.html

Neustaeter, Brooklyn. "Trump calls Trudeau 'far left lunatic,' expresses support for convoy". *CTV News.* February 5, 2022. https://www.ctvnews.ca/canada/trump-calls-trudeau-far-left-lunatic-expresses-support-for-convoy-1.5769394

"New Rations Book" Ad. *The Bancroft Times.* September 3, 1942.

Nietzsche, Friedrich Wilhelm. *Thus Spoke Zarathustra: A Book for All and*

None (1883-1885). Cambridge University Press. 2006

Pitas, Costas. "Trump vows new Canada, Mexico, China tariffs that threaten global trade". *Reuters.* November 26, 2024. https://www.reuters.com/world/us/trump-promises-25-tariff-products-mexico-canada-2024-11-25/

Plato. *The Republic* (2nd Edition, Translated by Desomond Lee). London: Penguin. 2007

"Project 2025: Mandate for Leadership – The Conservative Promise". *The Heritage Foundation.* April 2022. https://static.project2025.org/2025_MandateForLeadership_FULL.pdf

Proudfoot, Shannon. "Pierre Poilievre on his combative style of politics and his plans for Canada". *MacLean's.* April 2022. https://macleans.ca/politics/pierre-poilievre-on-his-combative-style-of-politics-and-his-plans-for-canada/

"Queen Elizabeth II has died". *BBC News.* September 8, 2022. https://www.bbc.com/news/uk-61585886

Rannard, Georgina; Poynting, Mark; Tauschinski, Jana; Dale, Becky. "Ocean heat record broken, with grim implications for the planet". *BBC News.* August 4, 2023. https://www.bbc.com/news/science-environment-66387537

Raycraft, Richard. "RCMP investigating rape threat against Pierre Poilievre's wife". *CBC News.* September 26, 2022. https://www.cbc.ca/news/politics/poilievre-threats-mackenzie-1.6595730

Richey, Dr. Rashad. "Anti-Vax Trucker Convoy REVEALS White Supremacist Views". *YouTube.* February 10, 2022. https://www.youtube.com/watch?v=WFFS0T2QwQU

Röbel, Sven; Wiedmann-Schmidt, Wolf. "Hanau-Anschlag – neues Gutachten zum Täter: Psychisch krank – und ein Rassist". *Der Spiegel.* November 27, 2020. https://www.spiegel.de/panorama/justiz/hanau-anschlag-neues-gutachten-zum-taeter-psychisch-krank-und-ein-rassist-a-00000000-0002-0001-0000-000174211404

Rodriguez, Robert and Maniquis, Ethan. "Machete Assassinates Robert Di Nero". Machete. Troublemaker. 2010. https://www.youtube.com/watch?v=IPtbTlvbpSc

"Arne and Nate", Photo by *Rose Bennett*, Nov 20th, 2024.

Rodriguez, Sofia. "WHO declares COVID-19 pandemic". *CBC News*. March 11, 2020. https://www.cbc.ca/news/canada/london/london-who-declares-coronavirus-pandemic-1.5494034

Roeloffs, Mary Whitfill. "Elon Musk's PAC Is Paying $47 For Each Solicited Petition Signature From A Swing State Voter—Here's Why It's Controversial". *Forbes*. October 7, 2024. https://www.forbes.com/sites/maryroeloffs/2024/10/07/elon-musks-pac-is-paying-47-for-each-solicited-petition-signature-from-a-swing-state-voter-heres-why-its-controversial/

Roosman, Arne. *Touching the Great Again: Visiting a Nursery*. Hannah's Lithography. March 2020.

Salinas, Rebecca; Ibañez, David. "21 killed in shooting at Uvalde elementary school shooting". *KSAT.com*. May 24, 2022. https://www.ksat.com/news/local/2022/05/24/active-shooter-reported-at-uvalde-elementary-school-district-says/

Samar, Kamuran. "Elon Musk sparks controversy in Germany over AfD endorsement". *Euronews*. December 21, 2024. https://www.euronews.com/2024/12/21/elon-musk-sparks-controversy-in-germany-over-afd-endorsement

Saramago, Jose. Caminho. *The Cave*. 2000.

Sarkar, Alisha Rahaman. "Netanyahu confirms he okayed Lebanon pager attacks that killed 40 and injured 3,000 people". *The Independent*. November 11, 2024. https://www.independent.co.uk/news/world/middle-east/benjamin-netanyahu-israel-lebanon-pager-attacks-b2644731.html

Shakur, Tupac. "The Rose That Grew from Concrete". *MTV Books*. 1989. ttps://allpoetry.com/The-Rose-That-Grew-From-Concrete

Shapiro, Emily; Brennan, David; Sarnoff, Leah; Reinstein, Julia; Deliso, Meredith; Pereira, Ivan; Geho, Lilia (video). "Hurricane Helene updates: Death toll surpasses 230 as rescue efforts continue". *ABC News*. October 7, 2024. https://abcnews.go.com/US/live-updates/hurricane-helene/?id=113931821#:~:text=Helene%20made%20landfall%20as%20a,26.&text=More%20than%20230%20people%20have,North%20Carolina%2C%20Virginia%20and%20Tennessee.

Shapiro, Emily and Hutchinson, Bill. "'Blizzard of Century': Death toll rises, military to enforce driving ban in Buffalo". *ABC News*. December 27, 2022. https://abcnews.go.com/US/20-dead-cold-weather-christmas-weekend/story?id=95809460

Shear, Michael D. "Live Updates: Biden Drops Out of Presidential Race, Endorses Harris". *The New York Times*. July 21, 2024. www.nytimes.com/live/2024/07/21/us/biden-drops-out-election

Smelle, Nate. "Boldly backwards". *Bancroft This Week*. April 28. 2020. https://www.bancroftthisweek.com/boldly-backwards/

Smelle, Nate. "DC's March for Science offers cosmic perspective on how science can save the world". *Now Magazine*. May 3, 2017. https://nowtoronto.com/news/dcs-march-for-science-offers-cosmic-perspective-on-how-science-can-save-the-world/

Smelle, Nate. "Local Smoke". *Bancroft This Week*. June 27, 2023. https://www.bancroftthisweek.com/local-smoke/

Smelle, Nate. "Roosman Touching Jazz". *Bancroft This Week*. October 1, 2019. https://www.bancroftthisweek.com/roosman-touching-jazz/

Smelle, Nate. "The Liar in Chief: Brock professor decodes Donald Trump". *The Voice of Pelham*. March 22, 2017. https://issuu.com/thevoiceofpelham/docs/the_voice_march_22_2017

"Spirits Rations" Ad. *The Bancroft Times*. October 5, 1944.

Spanish Government. "Actualización de datos del Gobierno de España" [Spanish Government data update]. *La Moncloa*. December 13, 2024. https://www.lamoncloa.gob.es/info-dana/Paginas/2024/131224-datos-seguimiento-actuaciones-gobierno.aspx

Stanley, Jason. "Buffalo shooting: how white replacement theory keeps inspiring mass murder". *The Guardian*. May 15, 2022. https://www.theguardian.com/commentisfree/2022/may/15/buffalo-shooting-white-replacement-theory-inspires-mass

"Stop the Menace" Ad. *The Bancroft Times*. February 26, 1942.

Strauss, Johann. "Kaiser-Walzer Op. 437 (Emperor Waltz)". *YouTube*. 1889. https://www.youtube.com/watch?v=LAVvBF7m260

"Storm Ana kills dozens in Malawi, Madagascar and Mozambique". *BBC News*. January 27, 2022. https://www.bbc.com/news/world-africa-60157537

Suzuki, David. *The Sacred Balance.* Greystone Books. 1997.

Tasker, John Paul. "Trump taunts Trudeau by calling him 'governor' of 'a great state'". *CBC.* December 10, 2024. www.cbc.ca/news/politics/trump-trudeau-governor-great-state-canada-1.7406226

Tenbarge, Kat; Chinchilla, Rudy. "Elon Musk announces $1M giveaway for voters who sign petition in battleground states". *NBC News.* October 18, 2024. https://www.nbcnews.com/tech/tech-news/elon-musk-raises-payment-offer-100-voters-sign-petition-rcna176075

"The legacy of Guernica". *BBC.* 26 April 26, 2007. news.bbc.co.uk/2/hi/europe/6583639.stm

"The insurrection televised". *The Economist.* June 11, 2022. https://www.economist.com/united-states/2022/06/07/the-january-6th-committee-is-about-to-reveal-its-findings

"The Wartime Prices and Trade Board" Ad, *The Bancroft Times.* August 16, 1945.

Thich Nhất Hạnh and Arnold Kotler. Random House Inc. *Peace Is Every Step: The Path of Mindfulness in Everyday Life.* 1991.

Thompson, Hunter S. "Fear & Loathing in America". *ESPN.* September 11th, 2001. https://proxy.espn.com/espn/page2/story?id=1250751

Thompson, Hunter S. *Kingdom of Fear: Loathsome Secrets of a Star-crossed Child in the Final Days of the American Century.* Penguin Books Limited. 2003.

Thunberg, Greta. *No One Is Too Small to Make a Difference.* Penguin Books. 2019.

"Two Dictators hold historic conference in Brenner Pass". *The Bancroft Times.* March 28, 1940.

"Two-year update. Protection of civilians: impact of hostilities on civilians since 24 February 2022". *Office of the UN High Commissioner for Human Rights.* February 21, 2024. ttps://ukraine.ohchr.org/en/two-year-update-protection-civilians-impact-hostilities-civilians-24-february-2022-EN

Trump, Donald J. "Donald Trump: I Love The Poorly Educated". *NBC News.* November 5, 2016. https://www.nbcnews.com/video/donald-trump-i-love-the-poorly-educated-630186051563

"Trump on Liz Cheney: 'Let's put her with a rifle standing there with nine barrels shooting at her'". *C-SPAN*. November 1, 2024. https://www.youtube.com/watch?v=6VHP68I2j2w

Tunney, Catharine. "Poilievre visits convoy camp, claims Trudeau is lying about 'everything'". *CBC News*. April 24, 2024. https://www.cbc.ca/news/politics/poilievre-trudeau-carbon-protest-alex-jones-diagolon-1.7183430

Twain, Mark. Charles Dudley Warner. *The Gilded Age: A Story of Today*. San Francisco: Hartford America Publishing Company, 1873.

Vandoorne, Saskya; Walsh, Nick Paton; Mezzofiore, Gianluca. "Massacre in Burkina Faso left 600 dead, double previous estimates, according to French security assessment". *CNN*. October 24, 2024. https://www.cnn.com/2024/10/04/africa/burkina-faso-massacre-600-dead-french-intel-intl/index.html

Villarreal, Daniel. "Hate Crimes Under Trump Surged Nearly 20 Percent Says FBI Report". *Newsweek*. November 16, 2020. https://www.newsweek.com/hate-crimes-under-trump-surged-nearly-20-percent-says-fbi-report-1547870

Voltaire. *Le Dîner du comte de Boulainvilliers: Premier-Troisième Entretien. - Pensées détachées de M. l'abbé de Saint-Pierre*. 1767.

"WATCH FULL EVENT: Trump speaks at National Association of Black Journalists conference in Chicago". *PBS Newshour*. July 31, 2024. https://www.youtube.com/watch?v=yjN5dvDTeaE

Waterhouse, James. "Why has Ukraine launched a cross-border attack on Russia?". *BBC News*. August 7, 2024. https://www.bbc.com/news/articles/c9d1yx9nwjxo

Wells-Barnett, Ida B. *Southern Horrors: Lynch Law in All Its Phases*. New York: The New York Age Print. 1892.

Wilkinson, Jonathan. "Future of Our Planet", *MacLean's*, April 2024. https://magazine.macleans.ca/macleans/macleans/2024-04-01ug

Woodward, Bob; Paikin, Steve. "Truth and Trump: An Evening with Bob Woodward". *TVO Today Live*. January 31, 2023. https://www.youtube.com/watch?v=5yBHNpKTIEE

Yee, Curtis; Santana, Rebecca; Whitehurst, Lindsay; Orsi, Peter. "Live updates: Shooter dead, rally attendee killed and Trump whisked off stage after gunshots ring out at rally". *Associated Press News*. July 13, 2024. https://apnews.com/article/trump-vp-vance-rubio-7c7ba6b99 b5f38d2d840ed95b2fdc3e5

Yost, Peter. "American Experience: Nazi Town, USA". *PBS*. January 23, 2024. https://www.pbs.org/wgbh/americanexperience/films/nazi-town-usa/

Yousafzai, Malala. *We Are Displaced: My Journey and Stories from Refugee Girls Around the World*. Little, Brown Books for Young Readers. 2019.

Ziady, Hanna. "Elon Musk says 'civil war is inevitable' as UK rocked by far-right riots. He's part of the problem". *CNN*. August 7, 2024. https://www.cnn.com/2024/08/06/tech/elon-musk-civil-war-uk-riots/index.html

Zwigoff, Terry. "Bad Santa". *Columbia Pictures*. 2003.

"The making of '*Twas a Sunny Day*", Photo by *Rose Bennett*, Nov 20th, 2024.

www.ingramcontent.com/pod-product-compliance
Lightning Source LLC
Chambersburg PA
CBHW022044020426
42335CB00012B/539